THIS BOOK WILL SHOW YOU HOW TO WRITE SUCCESSFUL TERM PAPERS FOR COURSES IN

ANTHROPOLOGY	HISTORY
ART	HUMANITIES
BUSINESS	JOURNALISM
CLASSICS	LAW
CONTEMPORARY	LITERATURE
CIVILIZATION	PHILOSOPHY
ECONOMICS	PSYCHOLOGY
EDUCATION	AND SOCIOLOGY
ENGLISH	RELIGION
GOVERNMENT	SCIENCE

And All Other Commonly Taught Academic Disciplines

ABOUT THE AUTHORS:

EUGENE EHRLICH is Senior Lecturer of the Department of English and Comparative Literature at Columbia University. He is chief editor of *The Oxford American Dictionary*, co-author with Gorton Carruth of *The Oxford Illustrated Literary Guide to the United States*, author of *Amo, Amas, Amat and More*, and the author of many other books.

DANIEL MURPHY is the editor of *Lady Gregory's Journals* Volumes I and II, and of the correspondence of John Quinn and Lady Gregory. He is preparing a selection of the correspondence of William Butler Yeats and Lady Gregory, and of Wilfred Scawen Blunt and Lady Gregory. Daniel Murphy is Professor of English at Baruch College, City University of New York.

WRITING AND RESEARCHING TERM PAPERS AND REPORTS:
A NEW GUIDE FOR STUDENTS

BY EUGENE EHRLICH AND DANIEL MURPHY

BANTAM BOOKS
TORONTO • NEW YORK • LONDON • SYDNEY • AUCKLAND

TO
Annie
Corky
Danny
Deidre
Dick
Jonny
Kate

WRITING AND RESEARCHING TERM PAPERS AND REPORTS:
A NEW GUIDE FOR STUDENTS
A Bantam Book / December 1964
28 printings through May 1985

Library of Congress Catalog Card Number: 64-7967

ISBN 0-553-22974-5

Published simultaneously in the United States and Canada

Bantam Books are published by Bantam Books, Inc. Its trade-
mark, consisting of the words "Bantam Books" and the por-
trayal of a rooster, is Registered in U.S. Patent and Trademark
Office and in other countries. Marca Registrada. Bantam
Books, Inc., 666 Fifth Avenue, New York, New York 10103.

PRINTED IN THE UNITED STATES OF AMERICA

H   37 36 35 34 33 32

TABLE OF CONTENTS

The authors wish to thank Bernard Kreissman, Director of Libraries at City College, who read and criticized the sections on the library and on reference books.

FOREWORD

Very early in your education, teachers will require
reports from you in various classes. In the sciences the
required report may be a description of a simple machine
or experiment—a homemade barometer, a doorbell, an
electromagnet, the hatching of a few chicks, a bacterial
culture, the analysis of a few drops of pond water. In the
social sciences the required report may deal with some
library research on a historical figure or event, interviews
with town officials, or the like. In the English class the
report will be of a book or a play, or perhaps a biographical study. As you advance in school, the research
tasks you undertake become increasingly complex, and
the reports reflect that increasing complexity.

If you ask a teacher why he assigns papers, he probably
will answer that a research paper teaches and demonstrates the ability to research, organize, and write a
competent and scholarly paper. This explanation may
sound a good deal like the catchall "It is good for you"
that covers studying Latin and eating oatmeal. In a real
sense, however, this explanation is completely correct.

First of all, any student who wants to do well in college
and every student who hopes to go on to graduate school
will have to be able to write research papers. But the
requirement of this kind of scholarship goes beyond
academic life. There is not a field of professional or
business life in the world today that does not demand
the ability to gather information, develop ideas, and write
well. In this sense, then, the research paper is a preparation for your future work. The scientist will spend much
of his life writing about his experiments—the New York
Times reported that Dr. William Carlos Williams, the

poet-physician, wrote more than 2000 papers in his long
career. The engineer is continually faced by the need for
writing report after report. The lawyer has his briefs,
which are based on library research.

But there is more to research and research writing than
its practical side. One must almost necessarily begin by
stating that research is rewarding. The library contains
man's recorded history. Nowhere else can you find so
much in so little space. By careful work, you can find in
books, manuscripts, newspapers, diaries, and letters any
aspect of this history. The enjoyment of the search is
great, and the writing itself is also enjoyable if you know
how to *think through, organize,* and *describe* what you
have found.

Another important reason for doing research papers is
that they enable you to go deeper into a field of study
than is possible in any other way. When you think of the
short time a course runs—fifteen or thirty weeks, a few
hours a week—you realize that a teacher can do little more
than scratch the surface of his subject. Add to the hours
of lecture and discussion the two or three books assigned
for reading during a semester, and you can see that the
total exposure to a subject is far from adequate. This is
especially true if the course is one you find interesting.

A research paper demonstrates your ability to do
scholarly work, teaches you how to study and think and
write, shows you where your abilities lie, and gives you
a chance to enjoy yourself.

USING THE LIBRARY

One of the first things you learn in school is that using the library is one of the most infuriating and enjoyable aspects of school life. You soon learn that you are going to spend much more time in the library than you had anticipated. You will soon find that if you are to keep up with your required reading, forge ahead with innumerable reference papers, and study adequately for examinations, the library will be your home away from home.

Libraries are usually divided into three general types: *technical,* a library devoted to some specialized subject for use in a particular field, such as the medical library in a large hospital; *circulating,* the library whose primary function is to circulate books to a diverse group of readers; and *reference.* It is with the general reference library, or the reference department of a library, that most students will deal throughout their school careers. In many large cities, the branch libraries are both circulating and reference libraries.

A reference library is a work place for scholars and students where they can read, study, and learn. The aim of a reference library is to be as complete in any field as is possible, and the result is an enormous number of books of which frequently only a single copy is in the library. It is simple to imagine what chaos results when many students require that same single copy at the same time for similar research topics. It is imperative, therefore, for you to know what you want in the library and how to find it. The following discussion will help you fulfill these two goals.

THE REFERENCE COLLECTION

Probably the first section of the library you will have to use is the general reference collection. It houses all the books that are not in such special collections as art, science, medicine, or rare books and manuscripts. In a large library the reference collection is usually serviced by a *Main Reference Room,* which normally contains the card catalogue—an alphabetical author, title, and subject index to all the books in the library's collection, including those in the special collections. The main reference room also contains a selection of basic reference books that are consulted so frequently that they are kept on shelves in the room itself. The call desk, over which books are issued when they are brought from the stacks in answer to a reader's request, is also located here. The great majority of the books in a large reference library are kept in the stacks, apart from the main reference room. The librarian (or librarians) in charge of the reference collection is stationed at the call desk.

The *Card Catalogue* is the key to the library's collection. It is an alphabetical file of 3-x-5 cards that lists all the books the library contains arranged by author, subject, and title. You will have to use the card catalogue throughout your school life, so you should familiarize yourself with the information the card contains. Intelligent use of the card catalogue will save you time and energy. The following is a discussion of how a card gets in the catalogue, and what the card contains.

Cataloguing a Book. When a library receives a book, it is sent to a cataloguer, who examines it, makes out a card that contains the author's name, his birth date, and if deceased, his death date, the title of the book, the publisher, place, and date of publication, the number of pages, and the size of the book in centimeters. The card also contains such information as whether the book contains maps, plates, illustrations, or a bibliography.

It is also the cataloguer's responsibility to determine the subject covered by the book and to give it a classmark that will enable the library to place it on a shelf with other books on the same subject. At the bottom of the

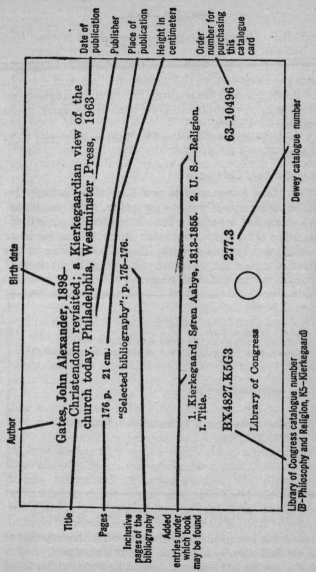

TYPICAL LIBRARY OF CONGRESS CATALOGUE CARD

Author

Birth date

Title

Pages

Inclusive pages of the bibliography

Added entries under which book may be found

Library of Congress catalogue number
(B-Philosophy and Religion, K5-Kierkegaard)

Dewey catalogue number

Date of publication

Publisher

Place of publication

Height in centimeters

Order number for purchasing this catalogue card

Gates, John Alexander, 1898–
    Christendom revisited; a Kierkegaardian view of the church today. Philadelphia, Westminster Press, 1963.
    176 p. 21 cm.
    "Selected bibliography": p. 175-176.

    1. Kierkegaard, Søren Aabye, 1813-1855. 2. U. S.—Religion.
    I. Title.

BX4827.K5G3   277.3   63–10496

        Library of Congress

3

card, the cataloguer indicates the subject entries that he believes will help a reader to locate the book if he does not know the author or title. Separate catalogue cards are made out for the author, the title, and the subject headings, and these cards are then inserted alphabetically in the catalogue. Only then is the book made available to readers.

A typical catalogue card, with all the main points indicated is shown on p. 3.

Using the Card Catalogue

The *Main Entry* card is one filed alphabetically by author, or by title if there is no author. From the librarian's viewpoint, whether a book is written by an individual author or by a group acting as author, the issuing body is considered the main entry. Thus Shakespeare, as the author of a play, is a main entry; so is the Government of Japan, as in this main entry card:

JAPAN. Geological survey.
   Chemical composition of volcanic rocks in Japan.
[Tokyo?] 1962.   xviii, 441 p.   (2 fold., col. issued in pocket)
27cm.

   In Japanese and English.

1. Rocks, Igneous—Japan. 2. Rocks—analysis. 3. Japanese literature—Science.

Note that brackets are used to enclose the presumed place of publication, which was not found in the book.

A work having so many authors or collaborators that it can be filed only by title, such as *The New York Times* or the *Encyclopedia Britannica,* would be found under those titles as main entries. Looking under the main entry is the simplest means of finding a book in a card catalogue.

Secondary Entries. In addition to the main entry cards

there are cards filed under a number of secondary entries, or "added" entries. These entries are "added" to the main entry to enable a reader to find the book if he does not know the main entry. The principal "added" entries are for subject, joint author or authors, title, editor, illustrator, translator, or compiler. Here is an added entry card for subject:

De Niverville, Louis   Copy only words underlined
                               & classmark   MAA

COLOMBO, JOHN ROBERT.
    Louis de Niverville.   (IN : <u>Canadian art.</u>   Ottawa.   30cm.
<u>v. 19, no. 2 (March/April, 1962)</u>   p. 144-145.   illus., port.)

1. De Niverville, Louis.

Notice that you would be able to find this biographical sketch by John Robert Colombo, even if you did not know the author, because Louis de Niverville has been added to the card as a subject entry. "Added" entries, such as this subject entry, are indispensable for the use of a library's collection.

Tracing. The "tracing" is a term used for the information placed at the bottom of the card by the cataloguer, which indicates what entries should be added to the main one. Normally the tracing is overlooked by students when they find a card in the catalogue. However, for a student who wants more material on a subject, the tracing contains valuable information. It lists the subject headings under which books on the same or related subjects are filed. Therefore it is a kind of key to the subject headings in the card catalogue.

When using a catalogue card, always look at the tracing. Then make a note of the appropriate subjects that might aid in further research. Go to the subject heading

in the card catalogue and check on the kinds and variety
of information available. Subject tracings are a great aid
in formulating working bibliographies and in determining
the extent of the library's holding in any subject field.
Here is a card that has a tracing giving the three "added"
entries under which cards for this book will be found:

```
                                               D-14
                                               1488

PEDERSEN, HOLGER, 1867-
    The discovery of language. linguistic science in
the nineteenth century; translated by John Webster
Spargo.   Bloomington, Indiana university press [1962,
c1931, 1959]   360 p.   illus., ports., maps.   21cm.
(Midland books. MB-40)

1. Philology--Hist.   2. Philology, Comparative--Hist.
3. Philologists.
                            ◯
```

The Card Catalogue Order. In order that catalogue
cards may be easily found, they are inserted in a catalogue
in a fixed order. Thus, if there is more than one title filed
under one author, the cards are arranged alphabetically
by title. Individual authors represented by both individual titles and collected works have cards filed in the
following order: collected works, individual works, works
edited by the author, works about the author, and bibliographies of the author's works (some libraries put the
bibliography first). It is worthwhile for a student to
remember this cataloguing order, for in the case of
authors such as Shakespeare, Benjamin Franklin, and
others very productive and interesting to scholars, there
is a great mass of material, and you can spend countless
hours searching in the wrong place for works by and
about such authors. Get familiar with the card catalogue—
it is the most useful and most used reference tool in the
library.

Subject Headings. Cards are also filed under selected
subject headings. Thus, the catalogue is in a sense a

subject bibliography covering an extraordinary number of fields. As you seek information about a subject, you will usually find that the catalogue can provide more material than you normally want. Since subject headings are often arbitrary and are certainly not all-inclusive, do not become discouraged if there is no entry for the subject you are looking for—ask the librarian for the proper subject entry. Do not waste precious time looking for something you cannot find after a reasonable search in the catalogue. When in doubt, *ask the librarian*—that's what he or she is there for.

Printed Card Catalogues. In addition to the catalogue that indicates the extent of the library's holdings, some libraries have printed catalogues in book form of the holdings of other libraries. These printed catalogues are invaluable as an extension of the library's collection, and should be used to determine what other works in the field, or by a specific author, exist. Often knowledge of the book's existence is the first step in locating it. The most notable and useful of these catalogues is the U. S. Library of Congress *National Union Catalog . . .* , which lists all the books in the vast collection of the Library of Congress and other cooperating libraries. The Library of Congress is one of the largest in the world, and the catalogue of printed cards (over one and a half million entries in 1940) is invaluable for determining whether a book exists, for establishing the correct title, or for other pertinent facts. If the book can be located in the Library of Congress catalogue, there may be information on the card that will enable the student to re-check the work in the catalogue of his own library and locate it. If his own library does not have the work and it is vitally needed for a paper, the student should inquire about inter-library loan (see pp. 11-12).

Another useful library catalogue in English is the printed catalogue of the British Museum, the national library of England.[1] It is similar in nature and intent to the Library of Congress printed catalogue. In general, this catalogue is of use only to graduate students, but all

---

[1] For a detailed description of both catalogues, see pp. 67-68.

students should be aware that it exists and should use it when other sources fail to produce a sought-after book.

Procedure. Searching for and locating books in a library of considerable size is no task to be undertaken in a leisurely and haphazard fashion. Consult the catalogue in some logical order—alphabetically by author, title, or subject. Skipping about from one part of the catalogue to another wastes time. If you know the author's name, look first under author, as it is the simplest of all entries to find in the catalogue. If you cannot find a book under the author's name but you know the title, check quickly for that; however, titles that are not distinctive are generally not catalogued, so do not waste too much time on the title. If neither the author nor the title is known, the book will have to be searched for under subject. *Get the correct subject heading*—don't waste time. Once the book has been located in the catalogue, fill out a call slip with the author, title, and classmark. The latter is located in either the upper left-hand or right-hand corner of the card. (See example on p. 6.)

Classmark. Two classmark systems are in general use in American libraries—the Dewey decimal system, used generally by public libraries; and the Library of Congress system, used frequently by college libraries. The Dewey decimal system has set up ten categories under which books are classified:

000 — General Works	500 — Natural Science
100 — Philosophy	600 — Useful Arts
200 — Religion	700 — Fine Arts
300 — Sociology	800 — Literature
400 — Philology	900 — History and Biography

The Library of Congress, by using the letters of the alphabet, divides its material into twenty categories. (I, O, W, X, and Y are not used, and E and F are both used for American History):

A — General Works	G — Geography,
B — Philosophy, Religion	Anthropology
C — History	H — Social Sciences
D — Foreign History	J — Political Science
E, F — American History	K — Law

L — Education	S — Agriculture
M — Music	T — Technology
N — Fine Arts	U — Military Science
P — Language and Literature	V — Naval Science
Q — Science	Z — Library Science,
R — Medicine	Bibliography

Open Shelves and Stacks

Although many libraries are not large enough to divide their collections into *open-shelf* books (books located in a room on open shelves where they may be consulted without using a call slip), and *stack* books (books shelved in a space to which access is normally obtained only with permission of the librarian), the great majority of libraries in which research is done do divide their books in this manner. You will soon encounter such libraries. Open-shelf books are those so frequently consulted that they are kept in the Reference Room. In the card catalogue the letter *R* or some other symbol precedes the classmark to designate a book that is on the open shelf. Encyclopedias, dictionaries, biographical indexes, atlases, periodicals, essays, book indexes, and other reference works frequently consulted are usually kept here. A special catalogue to this reference collection, indicating the shelf and press (aisle) where the work may be found, will help you find what you want. Familiarize yourself with this collection, for it will save much time searching the card catalogue for books that are perhaps at your elbow. Almost all basic reference books listed in the chapter on reference books (Chapter 9) will be found here.

Calling for a Book from the Stacks. Since it is both physically impossible and practically inadvisable for a library with a large collection to store all its books on open shelves, the great majority of its books are in the area called the stacks. Most often, in order to obtain a book from the stacks, you must fill out a *call slip*. In addition to your name, the call slip must contain the classmark, author, and title of the book. If there is more than one edition of the work—a specific edition of a play, for example—the publication date also must be given. The completely filled-out slip must then be presented at the appropriate place in the reference area, usually marked "Present slips here," or the like. Frequently you are given a number, and that number is written on your call slip. When the book arrives from the stacks, your number will be called or will be flashed on a board, and the book will then be delivered to you. Most libraries take from ten to twenty minutes to get a book to you from the stacks, so be prepared to spend that much time waiting for it.

If you have stack privileges, you will be able to go directly to the proper stack shelf and select a book, usually filling out a slip for it on the way out of the stack area. The one great advantage of using the stacks yourself rather than sending for a book is that, since books are shelved by subject, you can locate a number of books that are available on the subject on which you are working. It can be very frustrating to learn that the book or books you have requested by slip are in use, are in the bindery, or simply cannot be found. If your library grants stack privileges, *read the following carefully before entering the stacks*. It will save you many hours of fruitless searching.

Using Your Stack Privileges. Books in the stacks are shelved by classmark, and alphabetically by author within the classmark. *Don't go into the stacks without having first obtained the classmark, author, and title of the work you are looking for.* You won't be able to find anything. Look up the book in the card catalogue and make out a call slip—or a bibliography card—exactly as if you were going to hand it in at the call desk. This may seem a waste of time: you feel sure you can remember such a simple thing as a classmark during the time it takes to walk from the catalogue to the stacks—but *don't trust your memory*. You may meet a friend, decide to go for a coke, invert the numerical order in your mind, or do some other thing that will cause you to forget the correct classmark. Put the classmark, author, and title on a slip.

As soon as you enter the stack area, check the chart indicating the stack arrangement of books and note on your slip the stack and the press number in which the work will be found. Arrange your cards by stack and press number in some logical order that will not require long walks from one stack to another, or from one end of a stack to the other. Now you are ready to get your book. If the book is on the shelf—good; if it is not, don't leave the press immediately. Search the classmarks on both sides of the place in which the book should have been found. Perhaps the page or assistant librarian in charge of shelving the book misplaced it, or perhaps you will find another, equally useful book, shelved nearby.

If you don't find the book you want and cannot use another in its place, the following are some of the reasons it may not be on the shelf; in each case the librarian should be able to help you—but you will have to give him the classmark, author, and title:

- *In use.* If so, you may be able to put a reserve on it, which will give you preference when the book is returned. Normally a library will notify you by mail when the reserved book is returned.

- *In the bindery,* being repaired or rebound.

- *Lost.*

- *Ready for re-shelving.* Look on the shelf where books are sorted for re-shelving—you may be lucky and find what you want.

OTHER LIBRARY SERVICES

Use of Neighboring Libraries

If your school library does not have the book you are looking for, examine the collections of libraries in the vicinity. Do not become discouraged about finding a work and risk submitting your paper without proper documentation, only to learn too late that a library—public or private—in your area has the work. Every large city in the United States has a library system, many with several branch libraries. You should be familiar with these libraries and use them whenever the need arises.

Inter-library Loan

If you cannot find the work you want in your school library or in a nearby library, and it is not a work of fiction, it may be possible to obtain it by having your library borrow it from another library. Most major libraries will lend material to other libraries for the use of qualified students or faculty members for periods up to four weeks. Forms and information about this service can be obtained from the local or the school librarian.

Microfilm

A microfilm is a miniature photographic copy of a book, magazine, or newspaper—made either to conserve valuable library space or to acquire a work available in no other way. Microfilms have enabled libraries to extend their holdings enormously. Libraries can acquire copies of works long out of print, and can get complete files of newspapers and magazines—sometimes made by combining the holdings of several different libraries. A book you are seeking may be available on microfilm.

The librarian will show you how to use the microfilm reader. Once the machine has been set up and adjusted, it is as easy to work with microfilm as it is with the actual book, except that one cannot readily flip from page to page searching for a specific reference. Newspapers and magazines are more likely to be encountered on microfilm than are books. In the case of a newspaper or magazine, it is extremely important to have the exact citation, for searching for an article on microfilm is more tiring than searching in the original publication. Make certain of the year, month, week, or day; the page; and, in the case of a newspaper, the column. Put them on a bibliographic card—in addition to having them on the slip used to call for the book—for the call slip will not be returned.

CHAPTER 2

CHOOSING A SUBJECT

CRITERIA FOR SELECTION

There are three yardsticks for selecting a proper subject for research, and you must use all of them to arrive at the right subject:

1. You must be able to handle it.
2. You must want to do it.
3. It must satisfy your instructor.

Let us examine each of these in turn.

In deciding *whether you can handle a subject,* there are several considerations to keep in mind. First of all, any topic among the ones available requires a certain amount of prior knowledge. For example, you might undertake a Freudian explanation of the motivations of certain characters in a particular novel, or a consideration of the Keynesian influences in the management of money in certain modern industrial states. But the extent of your previous knowledge of the topic will have a great deal to do with your ability to handle it within a limited time.

Another consideration is the availability of source material. If you cannot find the sources needed for a given topic, there is little sense in tackling it.

Research papers often involve material not available in the typical school library. If you live or go to school in an area that has other libraries, the problem may be solved. But you must determine what you need early in the planning stage of your study, so that you can check all possible sources. Often all the materials you will need—books, magazines, newspapers—are available in the school or college library, or in area libraries. One note of warning:

these materials may exist in single copies, all in use by other students. Competition for scarce books can be time-wasting, even disastrous if you have put off your paper too long. The New York Public Library semiannually overflows with college students who spend their winter and spring vacations completing research they were not able to accomplish in their own college libraries.

Finally, you must have the time it will take to handle your topic. Some papers require an enormous amount of slow, careful reading; others require a great deal of writing.

In judging, then, whether or not you can handle a given topic, you must decide whether you have the background for the topic, whether everything you need is accessible, and whether you have the necessary time.

The second yardstick for judging the suitability of a topic is *whether you want to do it*.

You will research best and write best those papers that are interesting and exciting for you. Then all the steps in the procedure will be performed with zeal and enjoyment. Students fatigue fastest when they are bored. They work most slowly and reluctantly when they know they are going to be bored. You are well advised to forestall those unhappy situations by looking early and hard for a topic you will enjoy.

The last yardstick for selecting a topic is *whether it will satisfy your instructor*. Most instructors will keep in mind, when judging a topic submitted for approval, your ability to do a paper, based on your background and the availability of source material. This consideration will serve somewhat as a check on your judgment in choosing your topic. But the instructor has more than this in mind when he passes on a topic.

He wants to be certain the topic proposed is worthy of a term paper in his course. He takes into account the level of scholarship he expects from you, the areas for profitable study that exist, and the purposes for assigning a term paper. The topic you write on should be enough of a challenge to make the time spent worthwhile. The topic should be one that can be supervised by the teacher.

At the same time you study the topic you choose, you should also be learning about the procedures of research.

DEFINITION OF TOPIC AND THEME

Two terms will be used throughout the discussion that follows: *topic* and *theme*.

The *topic* is the field in which your research and writing will be done; the *theme* is the central statement you will make about the topic. The theme may be compared to the debater's statement: *Resolved that . . .* If you cannot put these famous words in front of what you conceive to be your theme, you do not have a theme. The theme is a hypothesis—a tentative statement—to be established or refuted by the research. In Chapter 4 theme statement will be considered more fully.

Thus, in looking for a topic for a paper in a course in government, you may be interested in comparing and contrasting the American and British governments. Obviously you cannot write a paper on this vast subject, because you would need more time than a student ever has, as well as a great deal of experience and insight. But perhaps there are areas within this subject that can be fruitfully investigated; for example, the comparative roles played by the House of Commons and the House of Representatives. As you think further, other possible topics will occur to you. One might be the methods of introducing legislation in the two bodies. Others would be the roles of political parties in the two bodies, responsibility of leadership, methods of election of members, recall of members, committee systems, and the like. Further thinking and reading follow to determine whether you can adequately research these topics. Finally the theme of the study will emerge.

FINDING RESEARCH TOPICS

In many courses, the teacher will suggest subjects for consideration by class members. He may even schedule conferences to help individual students. But most instruc-

tors, in suggesting subjects for research, will not propose
themes. That is your responsibility.

The best way to find a topic is to read quickly through
the specific sources of information your library provides
in the subject. Encyclopedias, handbooks, and bibliographies are the best sources. An excellent plan is to start
with the most general sources, and then to fill in from
the specialized sources available. Reading the broad
coverage of a field will give the student the benefit of the
scholar's overview of a subject that he should have in
order to understand just where his own, more limited,
topic fits in. Such works are fully described in Chapter 8.
If you have difficulty in locating these works, go to the
librarian for help. Soon enough you will begin to find
leads to all the references you need.

PRELIMINARY SEARCH

The preliminary search of sources has three goals:

- To select the topic you will develop thoroughly.
- To locate as many sources as possible.
- To verify that your research can be performed.

At this stage do not attempt to read carefully or to take
complete notes. Read here and there in each source, keep-
ing in mind that you are searching for a topic that can be
researched.

In preparing for a paper for a history course, for
example, you may be particularly interested in one of the
countries, periods, or phases of development. In a modern
European history course, it may be that your interest
lies in England, the Victorian Age, or the industrial
revolution. It is clear that none of them could be properly
explored in a single term paper. Within each of these
areas, however, are many topics that can be researched.
Just what is it that interests you in England, the Victorian
Age, or the industrial revolution? Is it the effect of
geographical isolation on the history of England during
the nineteenth century? Is it the relationship between
England's colonial policy and her commercial development? Is it the passage and impact of the Corn Laws?

You are now beginning to get down to topics you can handle. Even so, there is work to be done before you finally select a topic. It is quite apparent that these topics have to be limited further. Moreover, you must establish whether the library can provide the needed books and articles.

For another example, in an English literature course you can arrive at a topic by going from a particular period to a school of writers, a particular writer, a particular work, one aspect of that work. Several works can be compared in regard to a common idea, character, or attitude.

In both the examples used, a sensible way to proceed is to read the general articles on the subject in the major encyclopedias. In addition to an introduction to the subject, you will find a short, selective bibliography that will identify the most important authors and works in the field. At this point the library card catalogue is absolutely essential. It is an index of all the works your library provides.

The Working Bibliography

The working bibliography is your own list of works that you think might contain information you will need for your paper. It derives from your reading and your

BOOK

MARCHAM, FREDERICK GEORGE

A Constitutional History of Modern
England, 1485 to the Present. New York,
1960.

work with the card catalogue. Since the bibliography is tentative, 3-x-5 index cards should be used. For every book encountered, make out a card with the author's full name, the title of the work, and the place and date of publication. For each article, give the title of the article, the name of the journal, the volume number, and the inclusive pages of the article. Both types of cards are illustrated.

MAGAZINE ARTICLE

LEWIS, C. S.

"On Obstinacy in Belief," The Sewanee Review, LXIII, iv (October-December, 1956), 525-538.

It is important to make a card for every source consulted even if the source finally is not used in the paper. The working bibliography shows all useful sources consulted whether or not specific material is taken from them. If the working bibliography is kept faithfully, there will be no last minute rushing about to relocate sources.

The 5-x-8 Note Card. Once your topic has been selected and you have read some general works on the subject, the process of breaking the theme into several subdivisions begins. For example, for a character analysis of Falstaff in Shakespeare's *Henry IV*, you might want to subdivide this general topic into such areas as Falstaff's courage, his cowardice, his lying, and his relationship with Prince Hal. These tentative subdivisions should be listed on a sheet in your notebook. Whenever you encounter a source with material on one of these headings, make out a 5-x-8 note card with the subject heading and the author, title, and page of the source. If you find material that requires a new subject heading, list this in your notebook under tentative headings, and put the new subject heading on your 5-x-8 note card before you begin to take your notes. These tentative subject headings will become the main headings and sub-headings in your outline.

TAKING NOTES

The form of your notes is important. If you are going to be able to work well from your notes when you begin to write your paper, each note card must have a *subject heading* at the top. To avoid confusion as to source and the location of material within that source, *page numbers* of the reference must be recorded carefully, and *only one note should be taken on each 5-x-8 card*. All note cards with identical subject headings are kept clipped together, and the entire lot is kept in a file folder.

Reviewing Notes and Subject Headings. Notes should be checked frequently to make sure the necessary information is being obtained for each part of the research study. The theme itself may have to be modified if the tendency of the research material dictates that it should. The theme is developed from the material, and the theme must reflect the source; not the opposite.

Before starting work on a given day, preview all the subject headings you are researching so that you will recognize important information as it turns up.

Even though you have earmarked certain sources as particularly valuable for specific types of material, you may find useful information in them that pertains to a totally different subject heading. If you are familiar with all your subject headings you will be ready to recognize these windfalls and capitalize on them.

No matter how interesting you find a text, don't spend your time reading material outside the scope of your theme. Reading passages unrelated to your paper robs you of time you cannot spare, and may make completion of a paper impossible in the time allotted. Interesting side journeys in fascinating texts must be reserved for another time.

Read All Parts of a Source in One Sitting. Remember that some of the sources you read will be useful for more than one part of your paper. Cover all parts of those sources in one sitting if you can, so that you will not have to waste time in finding a particular title more than once. Obtaining a periodical or a book from library shelves eats up valuable time, and the only way to minimize this time loss is to read all parts of a source when it is in hand. Some large libraries provide individual study alcoves (carrels) for students doing research, and thus some source books can be kept for more than one day. Even so, it is good practice to get what is wanted quickly so that others may have access to the source.

Before stopping work on any given day, it is wise to look back over the notes taken to see that they can all be understood. If an error has been made in one or more of your notes, it will be easier to check immediately rather than to do so a week or two later. This advice applies to everything written on the 5-x-8 cards: *source*, *page numbers*, and *notes*. Verbatim notes are particularly to be checked, because the form of the language in which they are expressed may appear unfamiliar to you when you work over your notes in preparation for writing.

Before leaving the library, think over what you will do in the next library session. It is good practice to write a note covering what you intend to accomplish on your next library visit. One good way to save time in getting books is to make out slips, before quitting for the day, for the next sources to be consulted. Then, as soon as you arrive in the library, hand in your slips and go to the card catalogue to look up the books to be used either on that day or in subsequent sessions.

DIRECT QUOTATION, PARAPHRASE, COMMENTARY

Three kinds of notes are taken on your reading—direct quotations, paraphrases, and commentaries. Let us look at each of these and see how they can best be used.

Quote or Paraphrase

When you wish to report what an author has said,
you have a choice of quoting material verbatim, or making a brief summary, or abstract. Which technique you
choose depends on the use you plan to make of the
material and the language in which it is written. If an
important idea has been expressed so concisely that you
cannot possibly compress it further, or if its literary quality should not be impaired, then the exact language of
the original should be preserved in a direct quotation.

In doing research on the difference between poetry
and prose, you might want to quote some material from
Percy Bysshe Shelley's "A Defence of Poetry." Since the
distinction is succinctly stated there, a paraphrase would
probably be longer than the original, and less interest-
ingly stated. Material such as this should be quoted
verbatim:

> A poem is the very image of life expressed in the eternal
> truth. There is this difference between a story and a poem,
> that a story is a catalogue of detached facts, which have
> no other connection than time, place, circumstance, cause
> and effect; the other is the creation of actions according to
> the unchangeable forms of human nature, as existing in the
> mind of the Creator, which is itself the image of all other
> minds.

On the other hand, in preparing a paper on the personality of the creative artist, the student might read
Trilling's essay, "Art and Neurosis." Its first paragraph
reads:

> The question of the mental health of the artist has
> engaged the attention of our culture since the beginning
> of the Romantic Movement. Before that time it was com-
> monly said that the poet was "mad," but this was only a
> manner of speaking, a way of saying that the mind of
> the poet worked in different fashion from the mind of
> the philosopher; it had no real reference to the mental
> hygiene of the man who was the poet. But in the early
> nineteenth century, with the development of a more elab-
> orate psychology and a stricter and more literal view of

mental and emotional normality, the statement was more strictly and literally intended. So much so, indeed, that Charles Lamb, who knew something about madness at close quarters and a great deal about art, undertook to refute in his brilliant essay, "On the Sanity of True Genius," the idea that the exercise of the imagination was a kind of insanity. And some eighty years later, the idea having further entrenched itself, Bernard Shaw felt called upon to argue the sanity of art, but his cogency was of no more avail than Lamb's. In recent years the connection between art and mental illness has been formulated not only by those who are openly or covertly hostile to art, but also and more significantly by those who are most intensely partisan to it. The latter willingly and even eagerly accept the idea that the artist is mentally ill and go on to make his illness a condition of his power to tell the truth.

In making notes on this paragraph, you might paraphrase the opening sentence and include mention of Lamb and Shaw, or you might concentrate on the challenging final sentences for your notes. The choice would depend, of course, on the point the student wished to emphasize. But there is no doubt that paraphrasing or abstracting can be used. Full quotation in all probability would be inappropriate because of the length of the paragraph. You need to conserve the limited space available in your paper.

Incidentally, if you were doing a paper on the personality of the creative artist you might have overlooked the essays by Lamb and Shaw until Trilling pointed them out. As has been mentioned earlier, new sources of information are constantly uncovered as you proceed through your research.

Many more examples might be cited of cases in which you have the choice of quoting verbatim or paraphrasing. In reading for a paper on economics, for example, the student frequently encounters tables of statistical data. Such tables should be quoted in entirety only if all the items in them pertain to the specific topic the student is exploring. There is no point in wasting time in copying parts of tables that are not relevant to a study. A single line from the table may be all that is needed. An adaptation of the table can also be made, in which much of the material, or the entire table, is rearranged or restated to emphasize a particular phase of the findings. A summary in words, omitting numbers entirely, can sometimes give the essence of a table. For example, a table that details the economic growth of a country year by year may be summarized in a sentence that reflects the rate of that growth, and its upper and lower limits.

Commentary

The student's commentary on a source is the third kind of note mentioned. Frequently an author's attitude toward his material can be dealt with in a single sentence, phrase, or word.

As an example of how to do this, let us take a selection from John Hanning Speke's introduction to his volume, *The Discovery of the Source of the Nile* (Everyman's Library, 1937). Speke wrote this book to substantiate his claim to the discovery. It can be valuable source material for papers on many subjects: the geography of Africa, anthropology, colonialism, racism, Speke, the Speke-Burton controversy, self-determination, and the like.

The commentary is based on the following extract:

> How the negro has lived so many ages without advancing, seems marvellous, when all the countries surrounding Africa are so forward in comparison; and judging from the progressive state of the world, one is led to suppose that the African must soon either step out from his darkness, or be superseded by a being superior to himself. Could a government be formed for them like ours in India, they would be saved; but without it, I fear there is little chance; for at present the African neither can help himself nor will he be helped about by others, because his country is in such a constant state of turmoil he has too much anxiety on hand looking out for his food to think of anything else. As his fathers ever did, so does he.

Passages from this paragraph could be quoted directly in certain student papers, but the quickest and most effective way to deal with them for other purposes might be merely to refer to them in some fashion such as: "Speke's intolerant attitude toward Africans . . ." or "Still heard today are invalid arguments such as those made by Speke a hundred years ago, when he spoke of African characteristics." Such a sentence should be followed by appropriate citation of the pages and other bibliographic data needed to identify the source of Speke's original words.

To see how a research study can cite an entire book as substantiation for a point being made, with just half a paragraph in the study representing a full-length book, it is interesting to read these few lines from Beulah Ephron's *Emotional Difficulties in Reading* (New York, 1953):

> This fear of feeling what one really does feel—especially if the feeling is rage — is so prevalent that one must watch for it in every case. Almost everyone feels it is dangerous to be angry. An angry person is not a lovable person. An angry person will be punished for his anger. Someone will get back at him. No one can possibly like him. No one will want to be with him. He will be all alone. These are the frightening exaggerations that cause the true emotion to be forced out of awareness. It requires energy to keep it out of the way, to hold it back. Sometimes this effort is so fatiguing that little energy remains for work (1).

The reference (1) is to *Psychosomatic Medicine*, by Franz Alexander (New York, 1950), cited in Ephron's bibliography. The reader knows that this reference is made to substantiate the analytic interpretation by Ephron. She has brought the weight of a full-length book by a distinguished authority to the support of her discussion. The reader thus must assume that such an interpretation as she has developed has a background of support.

A paper may even cite many books or articles in support of a single point when the student wants to show that his idea has the backing of many authors. For example, in the book by Ephron, one sentence in the preface cites no fewer than thirty-seven published articles. Because all the articles are concerned with the same subject, it would have been wasteful to make individual references to each one.

In summary, the student may *quote* directly, *paraphrase*, or *comment* on what he finds in the sources searched. His choice of technique must be based on the use he intends to make of the material being cited. As long as he makes appropriate, complete, and accurate notes, never omitting vital bibliographic information, he can proceed through the careful reading portion of the research task. Periodically, as the work progresses, he must inspect his notes and theme statement to make sure he is finding the support he needs and to determine whether his theme statement remains valid. As he finds seemingly contradictory material, he must not ignore it, but must bring it into his study. Good research explains contradictions. When a student paper skirts the truth, the invariable result is devastating red-lining of the manuscript by the instructor.

EVALUATION OF SOURCES

Primary and Secondary Sources

Documentation for statements in a reference paper is usually supplied by references to sources. These sources may be either primary or secondary. A *primary source* is a first-hand record of an event. Thus newspaper accounts are usually primary sources. So, too, are autobiographies, collections of letters, and reports of experiments. A *secondary source* evaluates, criticizes, relates, or deals with primary source material. While primary sources have to be evaluated for the worth of the source—its validity, the intelligence and experience of the observer, or the accuracy of the report—secondary sources, since they involve the interpretation of the primary source by some individual, need even greater evaluation. The interpretation may be biased, inaccurate, or plainly incompetent; or it may be incisive, accurate, and invaluable. How can a student evaluate a source? If doubt exists about the worth of a source, follow this guide:

1. Evaluate the issuing body. In general the issuing body will be responsible for the validity of the work. The following are normally reliable:

- University presses of all major colleges and universities.
- Major publishing houses.
- Scholarly societies.

2. Find out who the author is, and what position he holds. Use one of the biographical aids suggested in the chapter on reference sources (Chapter 8). Also check the title page; sometimes an author's affiliation is recorded there.

3. Consult your teacher. He will usually be able to help.

Finally, familiarize yourself with the names of authorities frequently referred to in books you are working with. Usually they are eminent in their fields and can be trusted.

CHAPTER 4

FROM THEME STATEMENT TO OUTLINE

The actual writing of the research paper is drawing near. What started out as a broad area of learning has narrowed down to a specific topic within that area, and finally has pinpointed a theme to be studied and developed. Now you have completed all the necessary reading—with the possible exception of some last-minute discoveries. You have accumulated a body of notes in support of your position in the paper. What is the next step?

Prior to writing any paper of substance, an outline should be made, as a framework on which to build the structure of your writing. This is a means of organizing the presentation so that the reader can easily follow the argument being advanced.

Without an outline to work from, you will waste time in excessive, extensive rewriting. Although some rewriting is inevitable and productive in writing a paper of high quality, you can avoid much of this by juggling parts of your outline until you are satisfied with it. It is easier to reshape an outline than reorganize radically a complete manuscript.

The procedure for developing an outline for a paper is not difficult. An effective outline can take various forms, but it should contain three essential elements:

• Theme statement.
• Main ideas and supporting elements.
• Documentation sources.

This chapter explains these three elements of the outline.

THE THEME STATEMENT

What central thought has emerged from the research you have conducted? That central thought is called the *theme statement*. It summarizes in brief form the entire paper. Everything else in the paper will support it in some way—by expansion for emphasis, by explanation, documentation, or exemplification. The theme statement can be thought of, then, as an abstract of the entire paper. To put it another way, if all of the paper were lost except for one or two sentences, the sentences you would most want to survive would be the theme statement. In many papers, the theme statement becomes the opening sentences of the final paper; if it is not used as the actual opener, it comes soon thereafter.

Arriving at a Theme

Perhaps you have examined the relationship between two branches of a particular government. What can be said about that relationship in just one sentence? Here are three possibilities:

- In the political structure of Abracadabra, control of government expenditures rests not with the legislative officers of the state, elected by the people, but with the judiciary, appointed by the executive branch.
- The legislative body of Abracadabra, by virtue of its complete veto power, overshadows the executive branch.
- The relative strength of the legislative and executive branches of the Abracadabran government is determined by the individual strength of the men who hold office at any given time.

Any one of these theme statements might adequately summarize your research findings and define clearly the task to be accomplished in the writing of the paper. The main ideas and supporting elements needed to sustain one of these theme statements would then be arranged under it in logical and convincing order, complete with sources of documentation to be cited.

Or perhaps you have examined the life of a particular author to see whether some of the literary themes in the work of that author can be traced to events in his personal life. Here are three examples of theme statements for papers on such a topic:

- The social class to which Teargas belonged explains the attitudes expressed by his most sympathetic fictional characters.
- As a result of his early experiences, Teargas was unable in his novels to make his female characters more than cardboard people.
- The theme of spiritual despair characteristic of the novels of Teargas can be traced to the disillusionment he suffered in his youth.

Have you identified the literary themes of a particular poet? They can be stated in one sentence or a short paragraph.

Have you traced the rise of a particular movement in the history of a country? That rise can be summarized succinctly.

Have you surveyed the literature that explains a particular psychological phenomenon? The various explanations of the phenomenon can be briefly characterized and summarized.

Have you studied the effect of a particular social attitude on the development of the labor movement in a European country? That effect can be briefly stated.

The outline begins, then, with a brief but complete statement of the gist of what your research has produced. That statement is the key to the outline, the focus of the paper. Once that statement is written, each main idea and supporting element can be viewed in its relationship to the theme of the paper and to the outline on which the paper will be based. From that outline an effective paper will develop.

Main Ideas and Supporting Elements

How do you support statements in the paper? How do you convince a reader of the validity of a line of reasoning?

There are various patterns an outline may follow, depending on the nature and purpose of the paper to be written. A *historical* paper can be developed chronologically, or it can be developed by first thoroughly analyzing the most important events of an era and then discussing related side issues. A *biographical* paper can also be organized in both of these ways. Your choice of a basic pattern will depend on how you have viewed the life of your subject. The emphasis to be placed on events would determine the order of presentation. In a *literary* paper, you might trace a certain theme in the work of an author. It would be appropriate to state this theme and then trace it through the author's works, beginning with major works and finishing with minor works. Or the theme might be traced chronologically through the author's works. If you are dealing with the images in the work of an author, the central images might be dealt with first, and then the related images. In each case, illustrations from the author's work would be most appropriate. In an *analytical* paper dealing with a problem or event, the central issues should be presented first, followed by related side issues. Thus a crisis in the affairs of a state would be analyzed by dealing first with the most important aspects and then covering the less important.

SAMPLE OUTLINES

It is helpful to examine sample outlines to illustrate the various approaches that can be taken in developing some of the types of papers that have been described.

Ralph L. Powell is on the faculty of the School of International Service of American University. In his article, "Everyone a Soldier," written for *Foreign Affairs* (October 1960), he analyzed the origins and roles of the Chinese Communist people's militia. His sources were current literature and official documents of the Chinese People's Republic. Let us examine an outline we have prepared from the published article:

> *Theme Statement:* Under the slogan "Everyone a Soldier," the Chinese Communist leaders are militarizing the people by enrolling enormous numbers in the militia.

I. Build-up of militia exceeds Western concept of a nation in arms.
     A. The Chinese Communist Party is a militant organization, which has been at war during most of its existence.
     B. In 1927 peasant militia bands were first organized; militia grew to 5,500,000 by 1955.
     C. In 1958 a great drive began to increase militia at the same time as the "great leap forward" in production, formation of communes, and Quemoy Islands crisis.
     D. By end of 1958, estimates of militia ranged from 30,000,000 to 200,000,000, depending on state of training of militiamen.

II. Objectives of campaign seem to be more political and economic than military.
     A. Politics is in command.
         1. "Basic" troops constitute real standing reserve.
         2. "Ordinary" troops are an enormous labor corps.
     B. Economic roles of militia take precedence over military roles.
         1. Primary role is to aid in production.
         2. While it has important ties with the regular forces, its military training is still rudimentary.
     C. Effectiveness of militia is still far from satisfactory to Chinese Communist Party.

III. Ultimate objective of militia may be to guarantee survival in face of invasion or nuclear attack.
     A. Superior numbers hopefully will prove unconquerable by invading armies.
     B. Vast militia operating under widely dispersed, localized command hopefully will be capable

of carrying on, despite tremendous losses as
a result of nuclear attack.

This interesting and timely paper supports its theme
statement, which is a one-sentence presentation of the
gist of the paper, by three main ideas. Each main idea
is buttressed by supporting elements.

Before leaving the Powell article, it would be helpful
to read the first paragraph of the article. You will then
be able to see how the writer opens with the theme of
the entire article, giving his theme statement and indicating much of the structure of the article:

> Under the slogan "Everyone a Soldier," the Chinese
> Communist leaders are militarizing the people by enrolling
> immense numbers in the militia. This campaign exceeds
> the Western concept of a nation in arms, and is reminiscent
> of the proposals of the French revolutionaries or of Lenin.
> It is closely related to the "great leap forward" in economic
> development and to the regimented commune system.
> From a military standpoint, the massive training program
> has been described officially as creating a "human sea"
> or "steel wall." It also seeks to provide a highly dispersed
> defense against nuclear attack. The precipitate drive to
> create a "universal" militia demonstrates the supreme con-
> fidence and revolutionary zeal of the Communists. But it
> may be that they are also taking grave risks in creating
> localized, disciplined organizations and in training so
> many to use weapons of war.

An anthropology student might find that his reading
in one field would help him to write a paper in another.
He might, for instance, write a paper on the burial rites
among ancient peoples, using early writings and archaeo-
logical findings as source material. Here are the theme
and outline for such a paper:

> *Theme Statement:* Burial rites among the Greeks,
> the Egyptians, and the Anglo-Saxons differed in
> detail, but all three groups used cremation and
> interment, and the Egyptians and Anglo-Saxons
> both practiced ship burial.

I. Ancient Greeks usually burned their heroes.

    A. The *Iliad* recounts the cremation of Hector and Patroclus.
    B. Frequently the ashes of the dead were placed in urns.
    C. Other sections of the *Iliad* suggest interment.
       1. Erection of a barrow for Patroclus.
       2. Other evidence of the existence of barrows.
II. Egyptians interred their leaders.
    A. Pyramids presently exist in the Nile valley.
    B. Archaeologists have found burial ships.
III. Anglo-Saxons practiced interment, cremation, and ship burial.
    A. There is evidence of interment in *Beowulf*.
    B. In the same poem, Beowulf is burned on a huge pyre.
    C. The Sutton Hoo find reveals the existence of ship burial.

This outline is by country. The same paper could as easily have been arranged by the form of burial:

    I. Ship burial
   II. Interment
  III. Cremation

Charles A. Siepmann, of the New York University faculty, has written a book, *TV and Our School Crisis* (New York, 1958), in which he argues that the use of television in our schools will help solve some of our pressing educational problems.

In his first chapter, "Television and the Crisis of Our Times," he introduces his theme statement for the entire book:

> Education needs television because we have too few teachers for too many students . . . as bad as things are today, they are going to be worse still in the years immediately ahead. . . .

The bulk of the first chapter is devoted to tracing the trouble to two main causes: a sharp rise in the birthrate and a relative decrease in the supply of qualified teachers. He documents his theme from demographic and other types of sources. Here is how this first chapter might have been outlined:

> *Theme Statement:* We have too few teachers to-
> day, and the situation will grow steadily worse.
> I. A sharp rise in the birthrate has resulted in rapid
> overcrowding in our classrooms.
> II. At the same time, there has been a relative de-
> crease in the supply of qualified teachers.

With the support of well-documented sources, this argument is easily proved, and Siepmann moves on to present his television solution to the problem he has posed.

I. A. Richards, in an article entitled "Science and Poetry" (New York, 1926), claims that the recent acci-dental and intentional changes in man's customs and ways of life—the scientific revolution—will generate further changes in man's private and public life. Poetry that en-gages the mind and brings its various interests to com-plete equilibrium may be a means of ordering form out of this chaos.

His essay is in three main parts:

> I. Science since Galileo has changed the circum-
> stances of man's life.
> II. What then is valuable? That which engages the
> mind and brings its various interests to complete
> equilibrium is valuable. Poetry is a record of these
> moments of equilibrium.
> III. In order to function in the modern world, poetry
> must cut itself free from traditional systems of
> belief. If it does so, it may be the one moment of
> stability in the chaos that science may soon bring
> upon humanity.

Sentence Outlines

If we think of the outline as an aid in the actual writ-ing of a paper, it is important to have that outline in the most helpful form possible. For several reasons, the stu-dent benefits most from using sentences—rather than words, phrases, or cryptic abbreviations—for the major points of his paper. Minor elements can be cast as words or phrases.

Winston Churchill called the ordinary British sentence "a noble thing." It does not matter now whether he was overstating the case for the sentence, but it is clear that no important thought can be adequately conveyed in the English language by anything short of a sentence. Since the writing outline is a schematic representation of a complete argument, it is necessary that the main elements of that argument take the form of sentences. The theme statement established the burden of the entire paper; a complete sentence must also appear in each major division of the outline to establish the burden of each significant discussion.

Only when you have all the necessary sentences before you will you know clearly what you are going to be saying in your complete paper. The subject headings on your note sheets tell you what you will discuss in the paper, but they do not tell you what you will be saying about those subjects. Writing a sentence for each of the major parts of the outline commits you to a line of reasoning.

With your outline developed to this point, you can examine your line of reasoning. For *completeness:* has everything been discussed that ought to be discussed? For *cogency:* will the discussion convince the reader?

Seeing your material laid bare before you, you can work the paper through mentally before writing a first draft. You can examine the logic of your statements in the same way in which the teacher will examine that logic when the paper is submitted. If there are any gaps, you will be able to locate them and rearrange the elements of the outline or find additional material to fill the gaps.

Writing the paper, then, is a matter of composing the sentences and paragraphs in support of your ideas in the best possible form. With a sentence outline, you can concentrate on saying things effectively, rather than on finding something to say.

WRITING THE FIRST DRAFT

Some writers like to run off a first draft of an article or story as quickly as they can. They take no particular care with *how* they say what they say. While this technique may work well for some, it is not especially useful for the student research writer.

The writer gets ready for drafting his research paper by arranging all the tools he will need throughout his work:

- The *outline* is on the desk before him, along with paper, pencils, and typewriter.
- *Desk dictionary, writing handbook,* and *thesaurus,* or other word books are available, but beyond arm's length—preferably across the room from the student's desk.

Nothing else is needed or desirable.

BASIC REFERENCES

The choice of desk dictionary depends on your preference among the several fine dictionaries available, but a pocket dictionary will not suffice. What is needed is a work that can provide correct spellings and make clear the precise meanings of words in their various uses. A writing handbook will be useful in settling problems of sentence structure and other matters of style. Perrin's *Writer's Guide and Index to English* is a good example of this class of reference works especially suitable for mature students. A simpler book is the *College Handbook of Composition* by Wooley, Scott, and Bracher. Some students will find a thesaurus or book of synonyms useful. *Roget's The-*

saurus, Webster's Dictionary of Synonyms, and *Soule's
Dictionary of English Synonyms* may be used in conjunction with the desk dictionary to help find needed
words.

It must be emphasized that all these reference works
are to be used only after the first draft is complete. They
should not be consulted while the first draft is in progress,
lest they interrupt the development of the paper. For the
sake of a single word or a correction of a small stylistic
error, you may spend valuable minutes in side journeys
in these sources. Besides the time used in looking for the
desired word or grammatical rule, you may also find
yourself pursuing some of the other entries in your reference books. The best procedure to follow is to exhaust
your own ingenuity first and then leave a blank space
in your manuscript page if you come up with nothing
suitable from your own memory. When you have reached
the point in your writing where you feel you need a
break because the words have ceased coming, use this
break for looking up what you need from reference books.
It is far better to save all such problems until that time,
or even until the end of the first draft, than to be dis-
tracted from the main job on hand.

PROCEDURE

There is no rush to get through a first draft. Nothing
of importance will slip away if you have done your research properly. The outline and notes you have taken
on the 5-x-8 cards chart all the work that is ahead. You
will do more toward getting through your work on time
by working carefully through your first draft than you
will by rushing to complete a draft that will have to be
all but discarded because its quality is poor.

Where to Begin

The usual place to begin writing a paper is at the beginning. As you complete each part in correct order,
bear in mind what you have said and make notes of
material that will have to be cross-referenced, or picked

up, later in the paper. Yet beginning at the beginning is not necessarily the best procedure for all writers. Writing is a job that can reflect personal traits. You may be one of many students who have difficulty in getting started. You can often overcome that problem by writing first a part of the paper that seems easier to write than the beginning. The outline makes that feasible. Thus, you may want to leave the introduction of a paper for later and work first on a section of the body that you find less demanding.

Complete the First Draft First

The first draft should be completed before you undertake any rewriting. To begin to rewrite parts of a paper before the entire paper has been through a first draft is to risk spending considerable time on material that in the end may never find its way into the paper. A paper is an organic unit that must be read through on completion of its first draft to see whether it has succeeded in doing what it set out to do. No matter how careful your planning, how thorough your outline, the paper that emerges may turn out to do less than you had hoped and planned. It is better to find that out and make the necessary additions and deletions on finishing the first draft than to make time-consuming changes in that draft as it is being written, only to discard material later that has been reworked at great cost of time and effort. Rather than rework a part of a section that needs tightening, it is better to make notes covering the stylistic flaws that you see while you are writing.

Short Cuts

In working on the first draft, don't waste time copying material verbatim from your notes. The notes can be pasted or clipped into the paper where they are needed, or they can merely be referred to by keying the notes to the places in the text where they will be used. This applies to bibliographic references as well as to documentation. Keying can be accomplished by means of such notes as "quote verbatim #4," "use summary of #7," or merely "#12." This saves time and, perhaps more important, reduces the possibility of errors.

A valuable procedure in writing is to set a goal for each writing session. Before you begin, say to yourself that you will write a certain number of pages or complete a stipulated number of sections of your outline. You may even find that you can go further than you planned. But without a goal for each writing session, you will probably do less than you could have done.

In each writing session, before you begin to work look back at the parts of the outline you have already completed and then reread the part of the outline you are going to cover in that session. Be certain that you know just what you are trying to accomplish in the writing you are about to do. If you find there is need for some small revision that will strengthen the presentation, don't hesitate to make the change. As always, it is better to reconstruct an outline than to rework a complete paper.

In approaching the writing task for the day, treat each small unit of your paper as a single complete unit. Develop a series of well-constructed small papers that together will become a complete paper of high quality. Each of the smaller units—paragraphs and subsections— must have a beginning, a middle, and an end. Paragraphs are not loose collections of sentences strung together until the writer feels that the paragraph is long enough. A paragraph is not to be considered as either long or short—it is the development of the hypothesis contained in the topic sentence. The paragraph ends when the details in the paragraph prove to the reader that the statement in the topic sentence is valid. If you consider the function of the paragraph, you can make each sentence in it contribute effectively toward its accomplishment. You know from your outline or from your writing what the preceding subject was and what is going to be dealt with next. You know how each paragraph will have to blend with what has gone before and what will come after. Before starting a paragraph you must take all this into account. Only when you are clear on what you are attempting should you go ahead.

CHARACTERISTICS OF GOOD EXPOSITION

The writing that goes into a research paper must live up to the requirements of all good exposition: clarity, directness, and conciseness.

Obscure writing ends up intelligible only to other obscurity experts—sometimes not even to them. In 1963 a commission was established in the United States to try somehow to make the writing of social scientists clear. By casting the results of research in unaccustomedly simple and direct words, it was hoped that better understanding could be achieved among workers in allied fields. So it appears that not even experts can always fathom what an article by a fellow expert is driving at. When this happens, research effort has been largely wasted.

Every one of the many books on "how to write" give rules and suggestions for achieving clarity in writing. If such advice could accomplish what it set out to do, there would be no need for criticism or for courses in writing. The fact is that it is difficult to write clearly. Over a period of years, the student may reach this goal, but he must work at it constantly.

Among the suggestions often given for achieving clarity in writing is the use of an *outline*, and thus far in this book great emphasis has been placed on this technique. The outline helps the writer break his complex paper down into sections that are easily manageable by him, and are also intelligible to the reader. *Subtitles* can be used to help clarity. A *topic sentence* in every paragraph sets the reader correctly on course. *Limiting a paragraph* to one important thought is another help. Within sentences, *subjects and predicates* should be as close to each other as possible. *Pronouns* must be clearly understandable: to whom or to what do they refer? *Choice of words* that will say to the reader just what you want to say is another important help.

There is one other principle that can do much toward making writing clear: *Say exactly what you intend to say, no more and no less*. This means no hedging, no

"pretty" words, no jargon, no "trappings of scholarship."
Whatever thought you want to convey, say it; when it
has been said, go on to the next thought.

Using Quotations. A research paper is your work, and
your own words should predominate. What you utilize
from other sources should lend support, not constitute
the focus of the presentation itself.

Stringing quotations together usually reflects a writer's
failure to cull the material he has collected. Rather than
select only the documentary evidence needed to substantiate the theme statement of the paper, such a writer
gives everything he has found, making the same points
over and over again. One good quotation will make a
point; additional corroborative information should be
merely mentioned and cited. Take care, as you write, to
ensure that your paper presents a clearly evident point
of view—your own.

If you follow the principle of saying only what you
intend to say, no more and no less, you will write a paper
that is clear, direct, and concise.

CHAPTER 6

FROM FIRST DRAFT TO FINAL COPY

There comes a time in the writing of almost any research paper when the writer says to himself, "I am so tired of working on this thing that I will not spend another minute at it." The feeling is understandable, but you must resist the urge to quit work prematurely. The courage needed to stay with a manuscript through its final stages of preparation pays big dividends. There is work to be done, important work. The paper must be edited, perhaps rewritten in part, and then put into final form. This chapter deals with procedures for bringing the research paper through the last stages of the job.

If you are able to use a typewriter, type your first draft. If you are not, you will save time and improve the quality of the editing and rewriting you must do if you have a typist prepare a fair copy of your draft. Typewritten material is easy to read and easy to edit. You can act the part of merciless editor of your own work without feeling uncomfortable about cutting up your deathless prose. Besides, the vacation from writing while waiting for the typist will give you a better perspective on what you have written.

What kind of editing does the first draft demand? Structural and stylistic errors must be detected and corrected. Spelling, punctuation, capitalization, and syntax must be perfect, of course. It is even more important to examine the flow of ideas to see whether the reader can get from the paper what you thought you put into it. As you read this draft, be as critical as the teacher will be when the finished product is presented.

To polish his work, then, the student has three more roles to play:

- *Critic* sitting in judgment of whether the first draft has accomplished the purpose of the research.
- *Grammarian and stylist* seeing how the structure and expression of the first draft can be improved.
- *Proofreader of the final draft* making certain the paper to be submitted is perfect in all details.

Let us examine each of these roles.

READING AS CRITIC

Playing the role of critic is not easy for the student the first time he writes a paper, but the role becomes easier and easier to assume as experience accumulates. How should you evaluate a paper? Leaving matters of writing style aside for now and concentrating only on content, the first concern is mainly whether a paper takes a reasonable position and supports that position adequately. In performing this critical function, your teacher will usually read through a paper a first time just to see how the argument comes through to him. In determining whether the presentation is convincing, he first must be able to understand the point the paper is trying to make. He then must be convinced by the fairness and appropriateness of the supporting material developed to substantiate the theme. Knowing the scholarly field with which the paper is concerned, the teacher is able to tell whether supporting information has been cited fairly, whether all important sources have been covered, and whether the arrangement of the supporting evidence is as convincing as it can be. He can tell whether conflicting evidence has been ignored or whether it has been dealt with honestly. As you play this role of critic, ask yourself if the paper meets all these tests.

If the argument flows as smoothly as you thought it did when you prepared the outline, and if the presentation is as convincing as you can make it, then you have no more to do as critic of the paper. But if the first draft does not meet these standards, you must be willing to *rearrange the paper*, *go back to your sour[ce]* information, or even *search out additional re[sear]ch le[ads]*. These procedures may seem rather dreary prospects a[t] completion of a first draft, but if a paper has a fundamental weakness you must do whatever has to be done to correct it.

In reading as critic, it is best *not* to go through a first draft with pencil in hand. By avoiding the temptation to make corrections in expression, you have a better chance of seeing the paper as a whole, the way your teacher will first view it. After this reading is concluded, move onto your next job, knowing that you will now have to bear down on every paragraph, every sentence, every word.

READING AS GRAMMARIAN AND STYLIST

While it is easy to point out, as the preceding chapter has done, that good expository writing is clear, direct, and concise—it is not easy to meet these high standards. But if you are willing to sharpen your pencil and work ruthlessly on your first draft, you can do a great deal toward achieving an effective piece of writing.

The best way to proceed is to focus your attention on one section of your paper at a time, staying with it until you can do nothing more to improve it. When you are satisfied with it, go on to the next.

In examining a section, think of it as a complete unit that has its own stylistic requirements:

- Is there a logical beginning, middle, and end?
- Can the reader clearly see the main point it is making?
- Does each paragraph within the section have a logical structure?
- Has each paragraph a strong topic sentence?
- Does each sentence play an effective role in the development of the paragraph in which it is found?
- Is the use of the passive voice robbing sentence after sentence of vitality?
- Do too many sentences hang limply about the lifeless verb *to be*?

- Is every subject-predicate team clearly identifiable and in agreement in number?
- Is each word in every sentence the clearest, most precise, most informative word that can be found?
- Does the same catchall, feeble word appear in sentence after sentence where it can easily be replaced by one that says more?
- Does the dictionary agree that each word used means what the student thinks it means?
- Is every modifier used really necessary?
- Is every useful modifier close to what it modifies?
- Is there consistency of tense, voice, and person?
- Is every word spelled and capitalized correctly?
- Is every necessary mark of punctuation in place?
- Is all necessary bibliographic information in place?
- Are all bibliographic entries in correct and consistent form?

High school and college teachers demand that a research paper be free of errors in diction. Therefore you must not hesitate to work and rework every one of your sentences until they satisfactorily answer the questions listed above.

You may find it helpful to read a paper aloud as you edit it. By making sure that every word is heard as well as seen, you gain assurance that you have overlooked nothing in your struggle against ambiguity of thought and sloppiness of expression. If you know you are not a good speller, check the spelling of every word that looks at all doubtful. If punctuation is your greatest difficulty, review the section on punctuation in your composition manual before getting to work. The comma is the mark that troubles most students, and many reference books cover the use of the comma in a few pages. Reviewing the rules just before editing will surely save time and increase your chances of doing an effective job.

READING AS PROOFREADER

When you are satisfied that your paper is as good as you can make it, it is ready for final typing. Once the paper has been typed, the job of proofreading can begin.

No matter how careful your typist may be, yo are responsible for seeing that the paper you will hana in is in best possible form. Check every word in it once more to see that no errors have crept in. Errors in spelling, punctuation, capitalization, and sentence structure cannot be explained away by blaming the typist. Omitted words, lines, paragraphs, or pages mar many a student paper. Mistaken numbering of pages, errors in bibliographic form, or misspelling a teacher's name on the cover sheet must be caught and corrected. At this last stage of the lengthy procedure involved in writing a paper, spare no effort to make the paper as nearly perfect as possible. You have come a long way from the day when you first began to search for a topic. You have produced a research paper at the cost of weeks of study and writing. The paper stands alone, representing all that effort. A final hour's work is surely justifiable.

CHAPTER 7

FOOTNOTES AND BIBLIOGRAPHY

FOOTNOTING

It sometimes comes as a shock to students that material found in a book and utilized in a research paper has to be acknowledged in a footnote. But it is common courtesy as well as good research practice to cite the source of information that is not the student's own or is not common knowledge. The following discussion of footnoting practice is based on the general rules suggested by the *MLA Style Sheet,* published by the Modern Language Association (New York, 1951). Because some standardization is necessary in this field, footnoting and bibliographic practice that does not conform to the *MLA Style Sheet* will not be discussed. The citation of all sources usually encountered by students is, however, explained. The following discussion attempts to be as simple, clear, and accurate as the material will allow.

What Should Be Footnoted?

Every statement or concept that is not your own should be footnoted. That means there will be a citation for:

- Concepts quoted or paraphrased from another source.
- Facts or opinions found in another work.
- Ideas that have been of primary importance in the formulation of concepts.

Footnoting material quoted or paraphrased should not present a problem—*always* cite the source. However, there is some confusion about documenting ideas or opinions that were of value in a student's work. In gen-

eral, if ideas and opinions were formative in the paper—
if the paper would have been different had the student
not encountered them—then they must be cited. The student must be the judge in this matter. However, it is
better to err by being overzealous than to be accused
of laziness or ignorance.

In common practice there are two places where
sources are cited: in the body of the paper, or in a footnote. It is preferable, from the reader's viewpoint, to
have material cited in the text of the paper, since, with
this form of citation, he does not have to divert his attention from the paper. Here is a citation that has been
worked into the text of the paper:

> Arthur Griffith's *The United Irishman*, a nationalist paper
> and the forerunner of *Sinn Fein*, attacked the play (Oct.
> 17, 1903).

If the citation can be worked into the text without dis-
rupting the flow of the material, it should be. Frequently,
however, it is neither convenient nor practical to cite
sources in the text; in this case the source is cited in a
footnote placed at the bottom of the page or at the end
of the paper.

Footnote Numbers

All footnotes must be numbered, the number appearing
both in the text and at the point where the footnote is
placed. Number the footnotes consecutively throughout
the paper, using small Arabic numerals. Do not number
footnotes separately for each page, for any small revision
might change the manner in which material is arranged
on the page and necessitate retyping all the footnotes,
or even the entire paper. The footnote number should
be placed in the text at the end of the material cited,
and *after* the punctuation, if there is any. On a typewritten paper, roll the carriage back a single space and
place the footnote number between the double spaced
lines; thus, [1]. If the paper is handwritten, place the number slightly above the handwritten line. Do not use any
punctuation with the number—no period, no slash, dash,
or parenthesis.

If the footnote is placed at the bottom of the page, skip three lines after the last line of text, indent three spaces, roll back the roller slightly, and place the appropriate footnote number slightly above the line—but not as much as a line above. Footnotes are single-spaced, with double spaces between the footnotes. Do not use any punctuation after the footnote number. If the footnotes are to be placed at the end of the paper, use a separate sheet titled "Footnotes," and list the footnotes consecutively, following the same form as if they were at the bottom of the page—indented, single-spaced, with double spaces between the footnotes.

Footnote Form

Whenever you cite a work in a paper, you do it for the reader's benefit. Always keep the reader in mind and give him all the information he needs to find the book if he wants to do so.

Printed Books. For the *first* citation of a book, use the following form and order:

1. Author's name (or authors' names, in normal order, followed by a comma. Always give the name in the fullest form. Don't abbreviate the given name or names, unless the use of the abbreviations is normal:

   [wrong]   W. B. Jones
   [right]   William Bury Jones

but

   G. B. Shaw [Although this form would be acceptable since Shaw is well known, it would be better to write out the given names—George Bernard Shaw.]

2. Title of the work, *underscored,* followed by a comma, unless immediately followed by a parenthesis. Cite short titles in full. A long title may be abbreviated; however, always give the first few words of the title, and signify by the use of three dots that words have been omitted. Take the title from

the title page—not from the binding or the jacket, because these sometimes vary from the title page. If there is a subtitle, follow the title with a colon and underscore the subtitle. Capitalize the first word in a title and all other words except prepositions, articles, and conjunctions.

3. Place(s) and date(s) of publication, inclosed in parentheses, the place of publication followed by a comma. When the title page lists more than one place of publication, give the first place listed; however, if the home office of the publisher is known and that place appears on the title page, cite that as the place of publication. If the date is not given, use *n.d.*, or, if you find it some place in the book not readily apparent to a reader, enclose it in brackets.

4. Page reference, in Arabic numerals. For one page, use "p.", for more than one, "pp."

Sample Footnotes

ONE AUTHOR

[1]Aldous Huxley, *After Many a Summer Dies the Swan* (London, 1939), p. 67.
[2]Joseph Conrad, *Lord Jim* (New York, 1924), pp. 23-24.
[3]Graham Greene, *The Heart of the Matter* (Garden City, 1951), p. 109.

Citations for editor, translator, edition, more than one author, series, and other variations from the simplest footnote form are listed below under their appropriate heading. When a footnote must include any one of these citations, simply find the correct example and follow it exactly.

EDITOR

[4]*A Literary History of England*, ed. Albert C. Baugh (New York, 1948), p. 345.
[5]*Introduction to Aristotle*, ed. Richard McKeon (New York, 1947), p. 245.

TRANSLATOR

*Thomas Mann, *The Holy Sinner*, trans. H. T. Lowe-Porter (New York, 1951), p. 9.

'Charles Baudelaire, *Flowers of Evil*, trans. George Dillon and Edna St. Vincent Millay (New York, 1936), p. 25.

EDITION

*Cleanth Brooks and Robert Penn Warren, *Modern Rhetoric*, 2nd ed. (New York, 1949), p. 22.

*Edwin C. Woolley, Franklin W. Scott, and Frederick Bracher, *College Handbook of Composition*, 6th ed. (Boston, 1958), pp. 291-293.

VOLUMES

Note that when a volume number is given, the page reference is not preceded by *p*.

[10]Henry Osborn Taylor, *The Medieval Mind*, 4th ed. (London, 1930), I, 227-229.

[11]Felix E. Schelling, *Elizabethan Drama, 1558-1642* Boston, 1908), II, 163.

SERIES

Note that series references include *p*. before the page number; do not confuse a *series* or a *study* with a volume.

[12]*The Bhagavad Gita*, trans. Franklin Edgerton, Harvard Oriental Series, XXXIX (Cambridge, 1952), pp. 39-41. [Page numbers are included here since the series is used to collect a group of essentially unrelated texts—that is, it is not a volume number of this work.]

[13]H. M. Cummings, *The Indebtedness of Chaucer's Work to . . . Boccaccio*, University of Cincinnati Studies, No. 10 (Cincinnati, 1916), pp. 8-11.

Follow the form given above: if the volume cited is a *number* in a series, use Arabic (No. 10); if a *volume*, use Roman (XXIX).

TWO AUTHORS

When you cite a work by two authors, cite the authors as they appear on the title page of the book, and in the order in which they appear:

> [14]Cleanth Brooks and Robert Penn Warren, *Understanding Poetry* (New York, 1960), p. 2.
>
> [15]James Worth and William Weaver, *Past Is Present* (Paris, 1902), p. 133.

THREE AUTHORS

Cite as above, only precede the third author with , *and*.

> [16]Robert Stoddard, James Reilly, and Hayes Thomas.

MORE THAN THREE AUTHORS

The usual practice in citing a work by more than three authors is to cite the first author in normal order and add *et al.* (and others).

> [17]William Joyce *et al.*, *Family in the Bush* (Baltimore, 1923), p. 6.

ARTICLES IN BOOKS

An article in a book requires a citation for the author and title of the article and for the book in which it is found. Give the name of the author, title of the article *in quotes*, and then all the necessary information to identify the work in which the article was found:

> [18]Percy Bysshe Shelley, "A Defence of Poetry," *Criticism: The Foundation of Modern Literary Judgment*, ed. Mark Shorer, Josephine Miles, and Gordon McKenzie (New York, 1948), p. 456.

ARTICLES IN MAGAZINES

Citing an article in a magazine differs little from citing an article in a book. Usually the magazine has a volume number and a specific issue date—month, week, quarter

—that must be included in the footnote. It is imperative that the student record the volume number and the date when taking notes from a magazine—the citation for the magazine must contain both. As in books, the *p.* before the page reference is omitted whenever there is a volume number.

[19]Richard Ellmann, "The Limits of Joyce's Naturalism," *The Sewanee Review*, LXIII (Autumn 1955), 568.

[20]Ronald Singer, "Emerging Man in Africa," *Natural History*, LXXI (November 1962), 12.

[21]Joseph R. Dunlap, "The Typographical Shaw: GBS and the Revival of Printing," *Bulletin of the New York Public Library*, LXIV (October 1960), 535.

[22]Henry Miller, "Preface for the Power within Us," *Circle*, No. 5 (1945), p. 45. [Since no volume number is given in this periodical, *p.* before the page citation must be used. No. 5 is the issue number.]

NEWSPAPERS

Since most newspaper articles are unsigned, the only citation necessary is the name of the paper, date of publication, page, and, sometimes, the column number:

[23]*The New York Times*, June 16, 1924, p. 16:8.

[24]*The Gaelic American*, December 3, 1907, p. 3.

SUBSEQUENT REFERENCES, BOOKS

After the first reference, which contains the complete bibliographic reference, be as brief as clarity will permit in subsequent references to the same text. For most secondary citations, the author's last name and the page number will suffice. Here are typical initial and secondary references:

[25]William Butler Yeats, *Dramatis Personae* (New York, 1936), p. 51.

[26]Yeats, p. 57.

However, if more than one work by Yeats has been used in the text and cited in the footnotes, then the title of the work would also have to be included in subsequent footnotes to make the reference clear:

₂₅William Butler Yeats, *Dramatis Personae* (New York, 1936), p. 51.
₂₆William Butler Yeats, *The Letters of W. B. Yeats*, ed. Allan Wade (New York, 1955), p. 76.
₂₇Yeats, *Dramatis Personae*, p. 80.
₂₈Yeats, *Letters*, pp. 92-93.

THE USE OF IBID

Whenever a title of some length has to be repeated, *Ibid.* (Latin, *ibidem*, in the same place) may be used when references to the same work follow each other, with no other work intervening:

₃₁Yeats, *Dramatis Personae*, p. 42.
₃₂Yeats, *Four Plays for Dancers* (New York, 1921), p. 21.
₃₃George Saintsbury, *A Short History of English Literature* (New York, 1900), p. 21.
₃₄*Ibid.*, p. 29. [The reference here is *A Short History . . .*, since *ibid.* always refers to the work cited immediately above. However, the use of *ibid.* should be avoided whenever there would be no confusion if the footnote instead contained only the author's name.]

SUBSEQUENT REFERENCES, ARTICLES

Subsequent reference to articles is made by giving the author's name and the page reference, as in books:

₃₅Robert Penn Warren, "Knowledge and the Image of Man," *The Sewanee Review*, LXIII (Spring 1955), 187.
₃₆Warren, p. 188. [Here the reference is to the same article in the same journal. For another article by Warren, a new citation would have to be made.]

If two or more references to an article by the same author have been used in the text, the usual practice is to cite the journal in which the article appeared, rather than the title of the article:

₃₇Lawrence Durrell, *Justine* (New York, 1961), p. 41.
₃₈Lawrence Durrell, "Eight Aspects of Melissa," *Circle*, No. 9 (July 1946), p. 5.
₃₉Durrell, *Circle*, p. 3.

USE OF OTHER ABBREVIATIONS

Use of "op. cit." (*opere citato,* in the work cited) and "loc. cit." (*loco citato,* in the place cited): The writers of this book oppose the use of either of these Latin expressions. Such use usually does not save any time and sometimes causes confusion, especially if the work referred to by either term occurs on a preceding page. However, they are still in occasional use. Here are the situations in which they may be used appropriately:

> [40]Samuel Beckett, *Murphy* (New York, n.d.), p. 25.
> [41]Beckett, *op. cit.,* p. 47.

It should be noted that the abbreviation did not save any space in the example above—it used more space than the short form.

> [42]Richard Ellmann, "The Limits of Joyce's Naturalism," *The Sewanee Review,* LXIII (Autumn, 1955), 573.
> [43]*Loc. cit.* [The material will be found on the same page as referred to in the preceding citation. However, the author's surname and page reference would have served as well.]

Explanatory Footnotes

Material included in the text of a research paper frequently needs amplification or explanation that would seem inappropriate if it were included in the body of the paper. Material of this nature should be given in an explanatory footnote. There are two means of citing the source of the explanatory material:

1. By including the citation of the source in the text of the footnote:

> [44]In the Preface to *Parnell and His Party* (Oxford, 1957), Conor Cruise O'Brien writes: "To this day . . ."

2. By giving the citation at the end of the footnote:

> [45]This view is fully supported by a recent study by John R. Giggs. See particularly his discussion in *The Lost Individual* (New York, 1927), Chapter 7, pp. 88-94.

Remember that the footnotes are for the reader's benefit. Any more footnoting than is necessary to aid the reader is useless pedantry.

BIBLIOGRAPHY

The bibliography is an alphabetical list by author's last name of every work cited in the text or in the footnotes. In addition, a bibliography may include works that aided in formulating ideas but that were not cited in the text. The bibliography, therefore, *must* include every work referred to in the paper, but *may* include more. However, cite only those works that are relevant —not every book examined.

The author's name is placed flush against the left-hand margin and, if the entry runs for more than one line, the succeeding lines are indented three spaces. Entries in the bibliography are single-spaced, with double spaces between the entries.

ENTRY FOR BOOK

The bibliographic entry for a book differs in several ways from the form of a footnote. First, as noted above, the bibliography is an alphabetical list by the author's last name. Second, each part of the bibliographic entry —name, title, and place and date of publication—is separated by a period rather than a comma. Third, the place and date of publication are not enclosed in parentheses. Here is a typical bibliographical entry for a book:

Mudge, Isadore Gilbert. *Guide to Reference Books.* 6th ed. Chicago, 1936.

ENTRY FOR ARTICLE

Except that the author's last name comes first and is followed by a period rather than a comma, the form for a bibliographic entry for an article is similar to its footnote form. The only major difference—and a very important one—is that the bibliographic entry for an article must contain the *inclusive* pages of the article. The page on which you found your material is not enough. Here is the standard form for an article:

Spurgeon, Caroline F. E. "Imagery in the *Sir Thomas More Fragment*," *Review of English Studies*, VI (July 1930), 257-70.

The italicized (underlined if typewritten) section in the article title is the title of a printed book.

For more than one entry under the same author, omit the author's name and indicate the omission by a line about ⅓ inch long followed by a period immediately before the title. For an example, see below.

The bibliography should be labeled to indicate its nature. In most cases the word BIBLIOGRAPHY, centered at the top of the page and typed in capitals, is sufficient. If the bibliography is specialized in any way, indicate its nature: SELECTED BIBLIOGRAPHY, ANNOTATED BIBLIOGRAPHY (a bibliography with comments about the works cited), LIST OF WORKS CONSULTED, etc.

Sample Bibliography

Baines, Jocelyn. *Joseph Conrad, A Critical Biography.* London, 1960.

Beach, Sylvia. *Shakespeare and Company.* New York, 1959.

Blunt, Wilfrid Scawen. *Gordon at Khartoum.* London, 1911.

——. *Land War in Ireland.* London, 1912.

Coffey, Diarmid. *Douglas Hyde, President of Ireland.* Dublin, 1938.

Fay, William G. and Catherine Carswell. *Fays of the Abbey Theatre,* London, 1935 [Note that only the first author is given in reverse order. All other authors after the first cited have their names written in normal order.]

Gogarty, Oliver St. John. *Rolling Down the Lea.* London, 1950.

Harrison, Charles T. "The Poet as Witness," *The Sewanee Review,* LXIII (Autumn 1955), 539-550.

Hart, Alfred. "Vocabularies of Shakespeare's Plays," *Review of English Studies,* XIX (April 1943), 128-140.

Howe, P. P. *The Repertory Theatre.* New York, 1911.

John Quinn, 1870-1925, Collection of Paintings, Water Colors, Drawings and Sculpture. Huntington, 1924. [Note that with this title entry no editor has been listed, as none appears on the title page of the book. Since the name "John Quinn" is part of the title, it is not reversed and the entry is correctly placed under "J."]

Pound, Ezra. *The Letters of Ezra Pound, 1907-1941,* ed. D. D. Paige. New York, 1950.

Quinn, John. "James Joyce, A New Irish Novelist," *Vanity Fair,* VIII (March 1917), 49, 128. [Note that this article began on p. 49 and was completed on p. 128. The page numbers are therefore separated by a comma rather than a dash.]

——. "Modern Art from a Layman's Point of View," *Arts and Decoration,* III (March 1913), 155-158, 176.

Toksvig, Signe. "A Visit to Lady Gregory," *North American Review,* CCXIV (August 1921), 190-200.

Yeats, John Butler. *Letters to His Son W. B. Yeats and Others,* ed. Joseph Hone. New York, 1949.

Yeats, William Butler. *Letters of W. B. Yeats,* ed. Allan Wade. New York, 1954.

COMMON ABBREVIATIONS

The following list of common abbreviations is supplied to help your reading of scholarly papers, not to help your writing.

c., ca.	*circa,* about	No.	number
cf.	*confer,* compare	*op. cit.*	*opere citato,* in the work cited
cm.	centimeter		
ed.	editor, edition, edited by	p., pp.	page(s)
et al.	*et alii,* and others	passim	in different sections of the text; no page or pages cited
et seq.	*et sequens,* and the following		
f., ff.	the following page(s).	*q.v.*	*quod vide,* which see
		rev.	revised, revised by
fig.	figure	s.	series
ibid.	*ibidem,* in the same place	sic	thus. Used in brackets to indicate an apparent error was found thus in the original
il., illus.	illustration, illustrated by		
loc. cit.	*loco citato,* in the place cited		
		sup.	supplement(s)
MS, MSS	manuscript(s)	tr.	translation, translated by
n.d.	no date given		
n.s.	new series	vol., vols.	volume(s)

CHAPTER 8

TYPING THE RESEARCH PAPER

Although some research papers are written in long-hand, you will probably find it simpler and you will be more likely to get a better grade if the paper is typed. Whether you type the paper yourself or have it typed, the following standards will have to be observed:

- Use 8½-x-11 bond paper of 16- or 20-pound weight.
- Leave adequate margins.
- Clip or staple the paper at the top left-hand corner.
- Use a good ribbon and clean typewriter keys.

Size and Weight of Paper

The standard size paper is 8½-x-11, and can be found in most stationery stores. For the final copy, use either 16- or 20-pound bond paper. Your supplier or typist will know what these terms mean; however, you will know this type of paper if you have had any correspondence with a business firm or organization—it is the standard office letter paper. You will also want to keep a carbon copy of your paper; use onion skin for this. Use a good grade of carbon paper so that you get a good clean copy.

Margins

Margins are important to the teacher, if not to the student. The teacher will want to make comments in the margin of the text as well as on the title page, and to do so he will need adequate space. In order that the margins can be as fully used by the teacher as possible, clip or staple the paper in the upper left-hand corner so that the pages can be flipped easily. Stapling the paper along the left-hand margin makes the paper difficult to handle and prevents the teacher from writing there.

Begin the first page 3 to 4 inches from the top. For all other pages and for the other margins on the first page, leave 1½ inches at the left and top, and 1 inch at the right and bottom.

Pages are numbered consecutively, beginning with page 2. The first page is not numbered. Place the number about ½ inch from the top, at the right margin.

The Text

The text of the paper is double-spaced. *Footnotes* are single-spaced, with double spaces between separate footnotes. Entries in the *bibliography* are also single-spaced, with double spaces between the entries.

Indent each paragraph from three to five spaces.

Quotations

As a general rule, quotations of five or more typewritten lines should be separated from the text. Place a full colon after the final word in the text, indent five spaces, and type in single space, thus:

It has been observed before that images, however beautiful, though faithfully copied from nature, and as accurately represented in words, do not of themselves characterize the poet. They become proofs of original genius only as far as they are modified by a predominant passion. . . .

Quotations of less than five typewritten lines should be incorporated in the text using quotation marks.

Erasures

Strike-overs are not permitted in a term paper. All typing mistakes should be erased and retyped. This presents no problem if you are typing only one copy, but with a carbon copy you have to be careful. To erase an error, move the carriage as far from the middle of the typewriter as possible to avoid getting particles from the eraser into the typewriter's mechanism. Roll up the page a number of spaces and insert a 3-x-5 index card between the carbon paper and the carbon copy. You can then erase safely without smudging the carbon copy.

CHAPTER 9

BASIC REFERENCE BOOKS

The following list of basic reference books is inclusive enough so that a student doing a term paper in any field will find here the books he will need to get the job done. No attempt has been made to make this section a complete listing of all reference works. The student will, however, find here a list of basic reference works that will enable him to carry out a research assignment on almost any level of his school career. In the case of students whose research is more advanced or specialized than ordinary, Constance Winchell's *A Guide to Reference Books* should be consulted. The following list of reference works is based partially on that well-known work. All the books cited have been examined personally by the authors in the main reading room of the New York Public Library. *What is a reference book?* A reference book is one that either contains information constantly referred to—such as a dictionary or an encyclopedia—or one that directs a student to other works containing information—such as a card catalogue or a guide to periodical literature. Since this list of reference works is an annotated list—the use of each book is explained in a brief note—the student should be able to determine easily and quickly what kind of work he needs.

The reference books in this section are arranged as follows:

General Reference Works. Reference books that are indispensable for research in all areas—dictionaries, encyclopedias, guides to books and periodicals, general biographical works, and other such tools.

Specialized Works by Field. Reference books arranged

alphabetically according to special fields: Art, English, History, Psychology, etc. Under each heading the student will find the basic reference books necessary for doing research in that field.

Keep this arrangement in mind when using this section. If a topic in a special field is being researched, go to the books listed in the field of the research paper. If general information is sought—a biography, for example —look under biography in the section on general reference works.

The following is the arrangement of the general reference books:

> Periodicals
> Book reviews
> Newspapers
> Essays and General Literature
> Pamphlets
> Books
> Dictionaries
> Biographical Indexes
> Encyclopedias and Annuals
> Atlases

GENERAL REFERENCE WORKS

Periodicals

A periodical index is a reference work that indexes articles appearing in a group of selected periodicals (magazines) and lists these articles—usually under subject, title, and author's name. Such indexes enable readers to find articles in hundreds of magazines—both current and past—on any subject or by any author. They are among the most useful research tools. Here are the most important:

Poole's Index to Periodical Literature. An index to American and British periodicals for the period from 1802-1906. It is the standard source for magazine articles of the nineteenth century. It is a *subject index* only— there are no author or title entries, except for works that would come under no subject, such as a novel or a poem. Book reviews are indexed under subject; where there is no subject, under the author of the book. Anyone doing research in nineteenth-century magazines must use Poole's.

Reader's Guide to Periodical Literature. 1900-present. The standard twentieth-century guide to American periodical literature. It is issued monthly and semimonthly, cumulates into a one-year index, and then into indexes covering three to five years. It lists articles by author, subject, and title when it is distinctive. The *Reader's Guide* indexes approximately one hundred and thirty-five periodicals, mostly of a general nature. It is indispensable for research papers—general and non-technical.

International Index to Periodicals. 1907-present. A periodical index similar in form to the *Reader's Guide*, but covering more scholarly journals and some foreign periodicals. This is an important periodical index, and students should use it in conjunction with the *Reader's Guide*. Between them they cover the general and the scholarly—mainly humanistic—literature in periodicals from 1902-1907 to the present.

Index to the Little Magazines. 1949-present. An index to little magazines, primarily literary in scope, not covered by *Reader's Guide* or *International Index.* Since many important articles by well-known figures appear in the fifty-odd magazines indexed, this tool is indispensable to the humanities student.

Nineteenth Century Reader's Guide. Covers the period 1890-1899. An author, subject, and illustrator index to general and literary magazines. The *Guide* contains an index by title to about 13,000 poems.

Catholic Periodical Index. 1930-present. An author and subject index to a selected group of Catholic periodicals, mainly in the United States, Canada, England, and Ireland. Indexes a number of book reviews under author's name.

Annual Magazine Subject Index. 1907-1949. Contains an alphabetical *subject* index to over a hundred periodicals as of the last issue, mostly British and American.

There is some overlapping with both the *Reader's Guide* and the *International Index,* but the *Magazine Subject Index* covers many periodicals not covered by either, including the proceedings of local historical and antiquarian societies, etc.

Subject Index to Periodicals. 1917-1961. A quarterly subject index to several hundred British periodicals, including proceedings of academic and also historical and antiquarian societies; superseded in 1962 by the *British Humanities Index* and the *British Technology Index.*

In addition to these general periodical indexes, there are innumerable specialized indexes. Two typical indexes, given below, have been selected at random to indicate the nature and scope of such specialized indexes. However, the student should realize that these indexes are representative of the variety available in specialized areas, and check with the librarian or with a reference tool such as Winchell (p. 62) to determine if an index exists in the specialized area in which he is working.

Canadian Periodical Index, 1928-1947, and *Canadian Index to Periodicals and Documentary Films,* 1948-present. A monthly index to Canadian periodicals, with annual and larger cumulations.

Index to Selected Negro Periodicals. 1950-present. Indexes Negro periodicals not covered by other standard periodical indexes. Title changed in 1955 to *Index to Selected Periodicals.* Quarterly, with annual cumulations.

Union List of Serials. A catalogue giving the location and inclusive dates of the holdings of periodicals in American and Canadian libraries. Of great use to students, for by using the *Union List of Serials* one frequently can locate a periodical in a nearby library that the student's own library does not contain. The names and locations of libraries are indicated by a code following the name of the periodical. A key to the code is in the front of the volume.

Ulrich's Periodicals Directory. 1932-present. A classified guide to a selected list of current periodicals, foreign and domestic. Lists over 19,000 periodicals. Divided into subject fields.

Book Reviews and Digests

Book Review Digest. 1905-present. An annual index to reviews of books appearing in about seventy-five general periodicals. Indicates the periodical in which the review appeared, quotes from some reviews, and indicates whether review was favorable or not. Useful to indicate contemporary reception of a work and to locate reviews. Indexes general works—many scholarly and technical works are not included. In order to use this annual work, the publication date of the work being searched for must be obtained from the card catalogue, *Books in Print,* the Library of Congress *Catalog,* or some other such tool. No student should use this work as a substitute for forming his own judgment of the value of a work.

Newspapers

New York Times *Index.* 1894-1904, 1913-present. An index to the major news reported in the newspaper, giving date, page, and column number. Indispensable for fixing dates as an aid for further research, for biographical material, and for history and the social and political sciences. An alphabetical arrangement by individual and subject; issued annually. Every student should be familiar with this index.

London Times, *Official Index.* 1906-present. An annual index to the news and personalities in the *Times.* Stronger on Great Britain and the Colonies—and on Europe generally—than the New York *Times.* A very useful and important index.

New York Daily Tribune *Index.* 1875-1906. A brief but useful annual index for the period covered.

Gregory, Winifred. *American Newspapers,* 1921-1936. A union list of the newspaper holdings of American libraries, historical societies, private collections, etc., giving the extent of the holdings. Important for students living in large urban centers with more than one library, for by checking this list they may locate a nearby library that has an issue of a newspaper that the student's own library does not possess. For the same reason, the following work is also important:

Brigham, Clarence S. *History and Bibliography of American Newspapers*, 1690-1820. A union list, by towns and states, of the papers published during the period covered, giving the location and holdings of each newspaper. Gives historical information on the founding, editors, publishers, etc.

Essays

Essay and General Literature Index. 1900-present. An index to essays and articles published in books that normally have different titles. An indispensable index that does for essays and articles in books what *Reader's Guide* does for periodicals.

Pamphlets

Vertical File Service Catalogue. 1932-present. An annotated list of pamphlets, booklets, brochures, circulars, and charts, by subject, author, and title. This index is useful for students who want to do a complete search for material, for it includes advertising as well as propaganda and biased publications.

Books

The bibliographic tool for books is the library card catalogue (for a discussion of the information found on a card and the method of locating books by subject, see Chapter 1). Intelligent use of the card catalogue will solve much of the problem of finding books on specialized subjects. In addition, there are many sources for extending the scope of the library catalogue. Two of the major sources—the catalogues of the U. S. Library of Congress and the British Museum—have already been mentioned in the section on the use of the library. However, in order that these catalogues be used intelligently, a detailed description of them is necessary.

U. S. Library of Congress. *A Catalog of Books . . .* 1942. 165 vol. with supplements to bring the *Catalog* up to date. This catalogue contains—in card form—a list of all the books in the Library of Congress and other co-operating libraries. It is an author and main-entry list—there are no title or subject entries unless these are main entries. Each card contains the author's full name, birth date and death date if deceased, full bibliographic description of the book, subject headings, Library of Congress catalogue number, frequently the Dewey number, and often notes on the book's contents. The catalogue, as pointed out earlier, is invaluable for establishing whether a book exists; it is also a great aid in establishing an author's correct name and finding his dates as an aid in biographical work. Every student should be familiar with this catalogue of one of the world's great libraries.

——. *Subject Catalog*. 1950-present. A quarterly catalogue of the acquisitions indexed by subject. A generally useful supplement to the author catalogue. Annual and larger cumulations.

British Museum. Department of Printed Books. *Catalogue of Printed Books*. 1881-1900. A new edition, the *General Catalogue of Printed Books*, being issued alphabetically, is bringing the catalogue up to date.

The British Museum, like the Library of Congress, is the copyright library for its country. It has one of the most comprehensive collections of English publications in existence, as well as an extensive general collection. Should be used in conjunction with the Library of Congress catalogue to establish authors and titles, to fix dates, etc.

In addition to the two catalogues mentioned above, there are literally thousands of catalogues of private and public collections, both general and specialized. Anyone doing extensive work in a subject field will want to consult several of these catalogues. A partial list is in Winchell, pp. 9-11. See also Theodore Besterman, *A World Bibliography of Bibliographies* (Geneva, 1955). This work lists by subject any separately published bibliography. Has an extensive, separately printed index.

The following will also be found useful as aids in extending the collection of your own library:

United States Catalog. 1900-present. Continued currently under the title, *Cumulative Book Index* (*C.B.I.*).

An annual index to all books published in English, no matter what the country of origin. Published monthly, with annual and biennial cumulations. The *CBI* lists books under author, title, and subject, and hence is a great aid in searching for books in subject fields, or for finding the author of a book known only by subject or title.

Publishers' Trade List Annual. 1873-present. An annual author and subject index, by publisher, of books currently available. Both publisher and price are given for each book listed. Since the volume consists of a collection of publishers' catalogues, the information given about each book varies greatly. Since 1948 *Books in Print* has provided an author and title index to the *Trade List Annual*. It gives the publisher and price of a book if it is still in print, and refers the reader to the *Trade List Annual* if more information is needed. Useful for finding a book if only the title or author is known.

Paperbound Books in Print. 1955-present. An invaluable aid to the student wishing to own an inexpensive edition of a book he is using extensively for a paper. Lists both author and title of all paperbound books currently available. Issued quarterly.

Dictionaries

The dictionary is the source for information about word meanings, and is one of the books most frequently consulted by students. All students are familiar with such desk dictionaries as the *American College Dictionary*, or *Webster's New Collegiate Dictionary*, both excellent for their purpose. Because these works are so generally known, the following discussion of dictionaries will not include any of the familiar desk dictionaries. The following list is arranged from the most general to the most particular.

Oxford English Dictionary. 1933. 13 vol. Commonly referred to as the *O.E.D.* or the *N.E.D.* (New English Dictionary). The most authoritative and complete English dictionary. It is compiled on historical principles. The dictionary contains every word—except obscene words—used in English up to the time of its issue, tracing the word from its first use in English through all the changes in spelling, meaning, and usage. Each change is usually supported by a quotation from an English author. The dictionary is absolutely indispensable for anyone concerned with the meaning, spelling, and the usage of a word at a specific period. It traces all words except those that became obsolete by 1150. The book contains 414,825 words and 1,827,306 quotations. It is a wonderful source for historical quotations for all words included.

Sir William Craigie, *Dictionary of American English on Historical Principles*. 1959. 4 vol. A dictionary giving the meaning and date of all words originating in America from its colonization until the end of the nineteenth century. Words are accompanied by quotations, recording the first known use in America, with date. Corresponds to the O.E.D., above.

Funk and Wagnalls New Standard Dictionary. 1961. A comprehensive, unabridged dictionary of all words in current usage at the time of printing. The dictionary gives synonyms and antonyms for most words included, which is an important feature for students. Contains a list of disputed punctuations, foreign words and phrases, population statistics (now much out of date), and rules for spelling, punctuation, etc. Syllabication and Hyphenation are plainly marked, punctuation indicated. Contains approximately 450,000 words.

Webster's Third New International Dictionary. 1961. The most widely used and perhaps the most useful of the one-volume dictionaries. The definitions after each word are given in historical sequence. This edition added 100,000 new words or new meanings to its standard list and dropped many obsolete words. Introduction has rules for spelling, capitalization, and compounding; a guide to pronunciation, punctuation, and forms of address.

Webster's Dictionary of Synonyms. 1942. An alphabetical list of synonyms and antonyms. The dictionary carefully distinguishes between words of like meaning, illustrating the distinction with quotations from noted authors. The most useful dictionary of synonyms.

Roget's New International Thesaurus. 1962. A standard dictionary of synonyms, arranged under subject categories. Alphabetical index. Does not distinguish between words of like meaning, but does give a large number of synonyms. The number of cross references is helpful.

Skeat, Walter W. *A Concise Etymological Dictionary of the English Language.* 1956. A work arranged alphabetically that traces the source of most English words. Gives source, variations in spelling, etc.

Bartlett, John. *Familiar Quotations.* The best-known and one of the most useful and comprehensive works in its field. Arranged chronologically, with a very full index by word.

Also useful: Stevenson's *Home Book of Quotations,* Mencken's *New Dictionary of Quotations on Historical Principles,* Smith's *Oxford Dictionary of English Proverbs,* and other similar works. Do not forget that the *O.E.D.* includes nearly two million quotations, far more than any other work listed above.

Berrey, Lester and Melvin Van Den Bark. *The American Thesaurus of Slang.* 1942. A comprehensive and up-to-date dictionary of unconventional speech. Subject arrangement, with index.

Farmer, John Stephen and W. E. Henley. *Slang and Its Analogues. . . .* The most important and comprehensive slang dictionary, giving use, derivation, illustrative quotation, and synonyms in French, German, Spanish, and Italian, for over 100,000 words.

Wentworth, Harold and Stuart B. Flexner. *Dictionary of American Slang.* 1960. More than 20,000 entries—definitions and examples—from such sources as sports, underworld, military, and theater.

Partridge Eric. *A Dictionary of Slang and Unconventional English.* 1961. Includes colloquialisms, vulgarisms, catch-phrases, etc.

Biographical Indexes

All students are constantly involved with names—with who a person was (or is) and what he was famous for. Students are constantly seeking information about some author, historical figure, or scientist who has contributed to our knowledge in one way or another. Usually there is no other means for finding such information than going to a library and seeking information from some standard source. Frequently, however, when a student gets to the library, he finds so many entries that he can't determine which of them will be helpful. Here are some guides for finding biographical information with a minimum of effort:

- Determine whether the person is living or dead. For this the simplest procedure is to check the card catalogue. If the person is not listed or his dates not given, then check a biographical dictionary such as Lippincott or Webster (see below).
- Find the country of his birth, and if possible, the city or town.
- If he is living or recently deceased, note his occupation—scientist, architect, teacher, and so on.
- Go to the appropriate biographical index. If deceased, use for England the *Dictionary of National Biography;* for America, the *Dictionary of American Biography;* or other national biographies. If the person is alive, go to such sources as *Current Biography,* the *Biography Index,* or *Who's Who.*
- If the person is a specialist in some field, check for a biographical index in the field—the chances are one exists.

For convenience, the section below is divided into American, British, and International, and further subdivided into deceased and contemporary, as a great many of the biographical indexes are so divided. The indexes go from the general to the particular.

DECEASED AMERICAN

Dictionary of American Biography. 20 vol., with supplements. The most important biographical dictionary for deceased persons of note who lived in the United States. All the articles are written by experts, are signed, and have bibliographies. The *D.A.B.* is the first source to check after determining that the person is American and deceased. The *D.A.B.* is also a good source to consult for standard bibliographic material on a deceased person, as well as for the name of an authority who may be checked in the card catalogue for further biographical information. Arranged alphabetically.

National Cyclopaedia of American Biography. 1898-1962 (in progress). The most comprehensive American biographical index. However, the articles are not signed, and there are no bibliographies. The articles are written by staff members with the help of questionnaires and other information. Should be consulted if the person is not found in the *D.A.B.*, as the *National Cyclopaedia* is not as selective. The *National Cyclopaedia* also has a *Current Volume* that gives biographies for prominent living Americans. Both series are serviced by an index, the main volume by *White's Conspectus of American Biography.* 1937.

Appleton's Cyclopaedia of American Biography. 1887-1900. Generally superseded by the *D.A.B.*, but there are some persons listed in this out-of-print index who are not included in the *D.A.B.* Appleton's is also useful for the many portraits and for the signature facsimiles included with the articles.

Who Was Who in America. 1897-1960. An important biographical tool that includes biographical sketches removed because of death from the annual volumes of *Who's Who in America.* Each sketch gives the main outlines of the person's life and contributions.

CONTEMPORARY AMERICAN

Who's Who in America. 1899-present. An important biographical dictionary of notable living men and women. The first source to check for a living person noted either for his achievements or his official position. The coverage is broad and the biographical sketches are accurate.

Students should be aware of and use the large number of biographical dictionaries that treat individuals because of ethnic, religious, or professional reasons: *American Catholic Who's Who, Italian-American Who's Who, Who's Who in American Jewry, Who's Who in Colored*

America, Who's Who in the East, Who's Who in American Art, and *Who's Who in American Education,* among others.

Dictionary of National Biography (D.N.B.) Inclusive to 1950, the latest supplement. The most important source for eminent deceased persons in England and the Colonies. Excellent signed articles by specialists. Bibliographies cite the standard biographical study of the person. The primary reference tool for British biography.

Who Was Who. 1897-1960. A biographical index containing sketches of persons whose names have been removed from *Who's Who* because of death. Contains the biographical sketch originally printed in *Who's Who,* with the death date and, occasionally, new information.

Who's Who. 1849-present. A dictionary of living persons of note—principally British, but it also includes some persons of other nationalities. Contains accurate sketches; an important biographical tool.

Biography Index. Jan. 1946-present. A quarterly index to biographical material in current books in the English language, no matter what the country of origin; to biographical articles in 1500 periodicals; and to obituaries of national and international interest printed in the *New York Times.* The *Biography Index* is an invaluable tool for locating biographical material—it does not contain any. This index is most effectively used after the standard biographical sources have been checked, for it enables the student to keep abreast of the current biographical work being done on anyone in whom he is interested.

Chambers' Biographical Dictionary. 1961. A good general dictionary of the great of all nations from the earliest times to the present. There are 15,000 biographical sketches, many of which contain bibliographical references.

Webster's Biographical Dictionary. 1948. Sketches of more than 40,000 persons, some living; pronunciation of names indicated. Does not contain bibliographic references.

Current Biography. 1940-present. A biographical dictionary of persons of all nationalities of newsworthy attention. Published monthly, with annual cumulations. As each annual cumulation contains an index to the volume itself and to all preceding cumulations, the work can easily be used by consulting the index in the last bound volume and the current unbound monthly bulletins.

International Who's Who. 1935-present. Contains short biographical sketches in one alphabetical list, often only a few lines in length, of persons currently prominent in all the nations of the world. Complements national biographies.

World Biography. 1940-present. Alphabetical biographical dictionary of the *Who's Who* type. Short biographical sketches of eminent living artists, writers, officials, educators, scientists, lawyers, statesmen, etc.

Students should also remember that all good encyclopaedias are excellent sources of biographical information.

Encyclopedias and Annuals

The encyclopedia is one of the most useful and most used of reference tools. As the word implies, it is a summary of knowledge—a work in which one may find information about any subject. It is a storehouse of knowledge, and the first introduction to any field of research. In this section, only general encyclopedias will be dealt with. Where a specialized field has an encyclopedia devoted especially to the field—such as the *Encyclopaedia of the Social Sciences*—that work will be treated under the subject field. Therefore, in order to use this section correctly, one should check for a general work here, and then check under the subject field to determine that a work does or does not exist in the field. The encyclopedias here are listed according to their relative importance.

Use the encyclopedia as:

- The initial introduction to a subject or a person of importance.
- A source for a selected bibliography for a subject or a person.
- A source for a specialist in a field. Since most of the articles in the better encyclopedias are written by specialists, check the author of signed articles in the card catalogue. More often than not, he will have written other works on the subject.

Encyclopedia Americana. One of the most important encyclopedias in English. It is particularly strong on American topics, towns, and cities. The articles are authoritative, are signed, and have bibliographies. The encyclopedia is under continuous revision—some portion of it is revised for every printing, so the latest printing is to some extent a revised edition.

Encyclopaedia Britannica. Continuous revision. The most famous encyclopedia, and one of the best. The articles are signed and contain bibliographies. Until recently the *Britannica* was organized differently from other English encyclopedias—all the articles were long, important treatments of the subject written by outstanding specialists, and smaller subjects were treated as aspects of larger ones. For that reason the 9th and 11th (1911) editions of the *Britannica* are still important reference works for subjects in which recent knowledge is of little importance. Most libraries have one of these editions, and students should be familiar with the special qualities they possess.

Chambers' Encyclopaedia. 1950. A well-known British work with short articles on small subjects by recognized scholars. Many articles have bibliographies that list the standard works on the subject. Articles signed by initials.

Columbia Encyclopedia. 1963. A one-volume work useful for quick reference. There are about 70,000 separate entries, covering a large variety of fields. A large number of biographical sketches are given, with bibliographies.

The student should not overlook the many outstanding foreign encyclopedias—particularly if he has a second language. Even if he does not, the plates and illustrations in many foreign encyclopedias are superior to those in English ones. Listed below are some of the most noted of foreign encyclopedias, given as examples of what is available. The list is arbitrary, and is not meant to be inclusive.

FRENCH

La Grande Encyclopédie. 1886-1902. The most important French encyclopedia, and excellent by any standards. Out of date for current topics, but excellent for such topics as biography, history, art, and literature. Excellent bibliographies.

Encyclopédie Française. In progress, but a good number of the volumes are out in loose-leaf form. The work is being issued in subject areas, with an index for each volume.

Grand Larousse Encyclopédique. 1960-1963, in progress. To be issued in 10 volumes.

GERMAN

Brochaus' Konversations-Lexikon. 1928-1935. A standard German encyclopedia. Short articles on small subjects, with many illustrations. Good for German biography, literature, history. A new edition of this work is in progress, with many volumes now available.

Meyers Lexikon. 1936-1942, in progress. The latest revision of a standard German work.

ITALIAN

Enciclopedia Italiana di Scienze, Lettere ed Arti. 1929-1950. An outstanding encyclopedia. Excellent long articles, many illustrations, and a large number of excellent plates. The art illustrations are often the best available except for those in special art texts. All articles are signed, and most have bibliographies.

SPANISH

Enciclopedia Universal Ilustrada Europeo-Americana. 192?-1933. The standard Spanish work. Many detailed maps and plates. Long articles, bibliographies. Strong on Spanish-American subjects. Supplements bring the work up to date.

Most encyclopedias are somewhat outdated, even if a new edition is available, because of the time lag between writing, printing, and publishing. To fill in the gap, there are a number of annual reports on the major events of the year. When working with contemporary events or working on a particular year, consult one or more of the following:

Annual Register. 1758-present. A record of events, with chief emphasis on England and the Colonies. Good index. A very worthwhile and useful work because of its continuous publication from the middle of the eighteenth century. The *Annual Register* abstracts some speeches. Contains a necrological list (death list). Emphasis on history and politics.

Americana Annual. 1923-present. Serves as both an annual register of events and as a supplement to the *Encyclopedia Americana*. Contains biographies and necrology lists. Articles are signed.

Britannica Book of the Year. 1938-present. Serves as an annual survey and as a supplement to the *Encyclopaedia Britannica.* Signed articles. Some biography and an obituary list.

New International Year Book. 1907-present. An excellent authoritative record of the year's events. Many signed articles by specialists. Annual necrology list and numerous biographies.

Atlases

GENERAL

Atlases are extremely important research tools all too frequently overlooked. In addition to the obvious use for the location of countries, towns, and cities, they should be consulted to visualize the geographic location of events, to locate birthplaces, or to locate the scene in a novel, play, or other work. In addition to the geographical atlases, there are also historical atlases that deal with the events of each year—normally in chronological order.

Bartholomew, John, *Citizen's Atlas of the World.* 1944. A standard, well-known small atlas.

Cosmopolitan World Atlas. 1959. A good small atlas. Tables of areas, population, economic and political information, etc. Maps are by area rather than by country.

Life Pictorial Atlas of the World. 1961. A handsome work with a large number of beautiful drawings and photographs. Economic, political, and terrain maps. Population figures up to 1960, where available. Has an index to 75,000 place names. However, the atlas is not as detailed as it should be.

The Times Atlas of the World. 1955-(in progress). This new edition of a standard atlas is to be in five volumes. Aims to be as thorough as possible.

There are many other good small atlases, among them: Encyclopaedia Britannica *World Atlas* and C. S. Hammond, *Ambassador World Atlas* (1961).

Among standard atlases generally available at schools and colleges, *Goode's School Atlas* and Bartholomew's *Oxford Advanced Atlas* are standard works specifically designed for school use.

HISTORICAL

Bartholomew, John, *Literary and Historical Atlas.* 1913-1936. A set of four atlases grouped according to region, constitutes a gazetteer of places of literary or historical interest. Maps and places of battle, etc.

Cambridge Modern Historical Atlas. Covers the period 1490-1910.

Poole, Reginald Lane, *Historical Atlas of Modern Europe.* 1896-1902. One of the best historical atlases in English. Emphasis on British Isles.

Shepherd, William Robert. *Historical Atlas.* 1956. The standard smaller historical atlas. Covers the period 1450-1955.

Lord, Clifford and Elizabeth Lord. *Historical Atlas of the United States.* 1944. A widely used, inexpensive, good general atlas. The statistical tables are now out of date.

Paullin, Charles O. *Atlas of the Historical Geography of the United States.* The successive development and settlement of the United States. Immigration, financial development, boundaries at different periods, routes, etc.

The student should note that atlases are available in many subject fields. These specialized atlases are listed under the appropriate subject field.

SPECIALIZED WORKS BY FIELD

The following section is broken down alphabetically into subject fields. Under each subject field will be found the basic reference books that are most generally consulted and are most generally useful in that field. Students should not overlook, however, the general bibliographies and histories that often overlap another field—as anthropology and primitive art, philosophy and religion. Be certain to utilize properly all the resources available by checking the general bibliographies and histories in allied fields.

Unless the student knows very well what he is doing, he should not go directly to the basic reference books in a subject field, but to the general works—general encyclopedias, periodical directories—and determine how the topic or thesis fits into the general pattern by which subject fields are separated in the academic world. Determine what subject areas are likely to yield fruitful material. Look up the appropriate articles in a good general encyclopedia. Do a preliminary search in the card catalogue and the periodical and essay indexes. When you know what you want to do and what can be done, when the references in general works have been exhausted—go to the subject fields.

Anthropology

American Anthropologist. 1888-present. A bimonthly magazine that carries articles of interest in the field. Contains extensive book reviews and lists new publications in the field. An extremely important journal and research tool. A general index covers 1888-1958.

International Catalogue of Scientific Literature: P.1903-1919. An international bibliography of all important works for the period covered. Author and subject index. A most important tool, unfortunately somewhat dated.

Anthropology Today; An Encyclopedic Inventory. 1953.

A general survey of the problems in anthropology. Articles by scholars in this field. Good bibliographies.

Yearbook of Anthropology. 1955, 1956 (under the title *Current Anthropology*, ed. William Thomas). Articles by recognized authorities, with extensive bibliographies summarizing the recent scholarly work in anthropology. Lists dissertations in anthropology, as well as memorial lectures and the like.

International Bibliography of Social and Cultural Anthropology. 1955-present. An annual bibliography of the year's work in anthropology. Lists books, periodical articles, and essays for the field in general and by subject areas. Has author and subject index in both French and English.

Penniman, T. K. *A Hundred Years of Anthropology.* 1952. A general handbook to the field. Extensive bibliography.

Kardiner, Abraham and Edward Preble. *They Studied Man.* 1961. Contains brief critical sketches of twenty eminent anthropologists, with good bibliographies for each one.
See also: *Encyclopedia of the Social Sciences; Encyclopaedia of Religion and Ethics; Mythology of All Ages;* Frazer's *Golden Bough.*

Art

Chamberlin, Mary W. *Guide to Art Reference Books.* A subject guide to reference works in art. Includes an alphabetical index to 250 art periodicals of interest for art research.

Art Index. January 1929-present. A quarterly index to American and foreign periodicals, bulletins, annuals, in art, archaeology, arts and crafts, and related fields. A good, useful subject-and-author index, which includes an index to exhibitions and shows. Cumulated annually and triennially.

Index to 20th Century Artists. October 1933-April 1937. Each monthly issue contains detailed information about an artist: biographical data, works, museums exhibiting the artist, etc. Useful for the period covered.

Who's Who in Art. 1927-present. A biannual biographical directory of leading men and women in art.

Who's Who in American Art. 1936-1937–present. An annual biographical dictionary of contemporary artists. Contains brief sketches edited from questionnaires filled out by the artists.

American Art Annual. 1898-1948. An annual that includes, among other things, a biographical "Who's Who" (continued after 1937 by the *Who's Who in American Art,* above); scope, hours, and specialization of museums and associations; exhibitions; art schools and courses, etc. Continued by the *American Art Annual,* which follows the same general format.

Mallet, Daniel. *Mallet's Index of Artists.* 1948. An index to biographical material of artists of all nations and all periods, both in general reference and specialized works. A useful bibliographical tool. The Foreword must be read in order to use the work.

Year's Art. 1880-1947. An annual that discusses all matters of importance in the art world that occurred during the year.

Encyclopaedia of World Art. McGraw-Hill, 1959, in progress. Published in Italian and English. To be completed in 10 volumes. When finished, will be one of the most complete encyclopedias in English. Thousands of color and black-and-white plates.

Harper's Encyclopedia of Art. 2 vol. 1937. Contains short articles and brief bibliographies on all the major aspects of art. Contains biographies of living artists. Numerous illustrations.

The Pelican History of Art. 1953, in progress. Each volume treats the art of a different country or culture. Intended to cover, when completed, the entire field of art in all countries and cultures.

Upjohn, Everard, Paul Wingert, and Jane Mahler. *History of World Art.* 1949. A profusely illustrated survey of world art. There is a glossary of terms, a list of suggested readings, and chronological charts. Intended primarily as a college text.

Robb, David M. and J. J. Garrison. *Art in the Western World*. A useful one-volume work that includes a glossary, chronological tables, and a selected critical bibliography.

Cheney, Sheldon. *A New World History of Art*. 1956. A standard one-volume text. Contains a very useful annotated bibliography by schools.

Encyclopedia of Painting. 1955. Gives an over-all picture of painters, styles, and movements in world art. Alphabetical arrangement. Illustrated.

A work of outstanding scholarship and interest in art is in German: Thieme-Becker. *Allgemeines Lexikon der Bildenden Künstler*, 1907-1947. 36 vol. The most comprehensive work in the art field. Extensive biographies covering all periods. Contains selected bibliographies, brought up to date by: Vollmer, Hans, *Künstler-Lexikon*. A work that covers the twentieth century.

Students in art will also wish to consult the magnificent plates in the *Enciclopedia Italiana*. This can be done for schools and movements by checking the Italian terms in an English-Italian dictionary.

Economics

International Bibliography of Economics. 1952-present. An annual bibliography of all publications in the general field of economics—arranged by classes, with author and geographical indexes. A most important research tool.

Economic Abstracts. 1952-   . Abstract articles on economics in about seventy-five periodicals.

Hasse, Adelaide. *Index of Economic Material in Documents of the States of the United States*. 1907-1922. A comprehensive report of all material on economics found in state documents. Gives exact reference to volume and page. Not all states covered. No longer published.

Oxford University Press. *Oxford Economic Atlas of the World*. 1959. Supplies basic information about world economics. Two parts—one part maps, the other an index and statistical report.

———. *Oxford Regional Economic Atlas* (in progress).

Separate atlases to cover the Middle East and North Africa, Africa, Soviet Union and Eastern Europe, etc.

Education

Monroe, Walter Scott and Louis Shores. *Bibliographies and Summaries in Education to July 1935.* An alphabetical subject and author list to more than 4000 annotated bibliographies and summaries.

Education Index. 1929-present. A monthly subject and author index to educational literature in over 150 periodicals, annual and triennial cumulations. Book reviews and poems are listed separately under those headings.

Encyclopedia of Educational Research. 1960, ed. Chester W. Harris. A guide to the literature of educational research arranged alphabetically. Long selective bibliographies and signed articles. A useful handbook.

Good, Carter Victor. *Dictionary of Education.* 1959. A dictionary defining about 20,000 terms used in the field of education.

Monroe, Paul. *Cyclopedia of Education.* 1918-1919. A general encyclopedia of education in all periods and all countries, with special emphasis on United States. Has signed articles with bibliographies. Now unfortunately out of date, but excellent for the period covered.

United Nations Educational, Scientific, and Cultural Organization. Education Clearing House. *Education Abstracts.* 1949-present. A monthly abstract, each issue of which is devoted to a different aspect of education.

Who's Who in American Education. 1928-present. Contains brief biographical sketches of everyone important in education.

Cattell, Jaques. *American Men of Science.* 1960- . 15 vol. 10 ed. Brief biographical sketches of approximately 120,000 persons in the physical, biological, social, and behavioral sciences.

Cattell, Jaques and E. E. Ross. *Leaders in Education.* 1948. Contains brief biographical sketches of over 16,000 individual administrators in education, such as deans and presidents.

Cattell, Jaques. *Directory of American Scholars*. 1957. Contains brief biographical sketches of some 12,000 scholars in the social sciences and the humanities.

History

This section on history will be divided, like Gaul, into three parts: General, American, and European, including classical Greek and Roman.

GENERAL

American Historical Association. *Guide to Historical Literature*. 1961. An annotated bibliography of historical works, divided by country or section (i.e., Medieval Europe).

Coulter, Edith and Melanie Gerstenfeld. *Historical Bibliographies*. 1935. A selective list of current and retrospective bibliographies. Useful, but somewhat out of date.

Documents on International Affairs. Annual. 1928-present. Topical arrangement. As the title indicates, this important work prints the important documents—letters, statutes, resolutions—in international affairs each year.

Frewer, Louis B. *Bibliography of Historical Writings Published in Great Britain and the Empire, 1940-1945*. 1947. Divided into subject areas (i.e., religious history), country, and period. Alphabetical within each category.

Lancaster, Joan. *Bibliography of Historical Works Issued in the United Kingdom, 1946-1956*. 1957. Arranged by country. Similar to Frewer above.

Historical Abstracts, 1775-1945. 1955-1959. A quarterly that abstracts articles of historical interest from 300 to 400 current periodicals. International in scope.

AMERICAN

Beers, Henry P. *Bibliographies in American History*. 1942. A classified list, with author and subject index, of over 11,000 bibliographies in American history. Divided

86 **Basic Reference Books**

into general subjects and the states and territories. A most useful work.

Writings on American History. 1902-present. An extremely important and useful annual bibliography and index to publications in American history. Contains annotated descriptive and content notes, and refers to critical reviews. Indexes anything of importance for study and research pertaining to the history of the United States published anywhere. Author, title, and subject index.

Dictionary of American History. 1942. 5 vol., index, and supplement (1961). Contains brief signed articles on all aspects of American history. Each article refers to one or two well-known works dealing with the subject. A very useful work.

Harper's Encyclopedia of United States History from 458 A.D. to 1912. 1912. 10 vol. A useful work for the period covered. Now much out of date. Contains a great deal of bibliographical information. No bibliographies or signed articles.

American Nation: a History from Original Sources. 1904-1918. 28 vol. A standard history, each volume written by a different scholar. Extensive bibliographies.

Handlin, Oscar, *et al. Harvard Guide to American History.* 1955. Two sections: first has sixty-six essays dealing with the methods, resources, and materials of American history; the second section is a detailed reading list arranged with reference to historical periods. A useful and much used work.

Mugridge, Donald and Blanche P. McCrum. *A Guide to the Study of the United States of America.* 1960. A selected, often annotated, list of books dealing with important Americans and all aspects of American history. An excellent work that prefaces each section with a short article. Indispensable work of outstanding quality.

American Historical Review. Oct. 1895-date. Quarterly. Contains detailed reviews of books on American history.

Morris, Richard B. *Encyclopedia of American History.* 1961. Divided into two sections: basic chronology of the development, and a typical chronology. Contains an in-

dex to 400 notable Americans. An excellent one-volume
work.

GREEK AND ROMAN

In addition to the works listed below, see also the several works listed under Literature, Classical, p. 89.

Smith, William. *Dictionary of Greek and Roman Biography and Mythology.* 1880. 3 vol. A standard work, now
out of date, but still useful where modern developments
are not important.

Smith, William, William Wayt, and G. E. Marindin,
Dictionary of Greek and Roman Antiquities. 1890-1891.
2 vol. Very much out of date, but still useful where modern research is not important.

Cambridge Ancient History. 1923-1939. 12 vol., and 5
vol. of plates and maps. The standard history of the period
in English. Each chapter written by one or more specialists, with full bibliographies and indexes.

Grundy, George B. *Murray's Small Classical Atlas.*
1917.

MEDIEVAL

Cambridge Medieval History. 1957-1959. 8 vol. The
standard work for the field. Each chapter written by specialists with full bibliographies.

Williams, Harry F. *An Index of Mediaeval Studies Published in Festschriften,* 1865-1946. 1951. An index of articles found in works written in honor of some person or
occasion. Indexes some 5000 articles in about 500 works.
Subject and author index, index to Festschriften, and reviews of Festschriften.

*Progress of Medieval and Renaissance Studies in the
United States and Canada.* 1923-present. Contains a list
of medievalists and their publications, and a list of doc-
toral dissertations.

MODERN

Cambridge Modern History. 1902-1926. 13 vol. and

atlas. The standard modern history. Extremely useful. Full bibliographies.

New Cambridge Modern History. Similar in scope to the original work above; however, the *New Cambridge Modern History* has no bibliography and no footnotes, so the old edition must be consulted for these important tools.

BRITISH

Bouser, Wilfrid. *An Anglo-Saxon and Celtic Bibliography.* (450-1087). 2 vol. 1957. An exhaustive bibliography of books, articles, journals, etc., by topic. Vol. 2 is an author and subject index. A valuable work for the period covered. Does not treat art or literature.

Gross, Charles. *Sources and Literature of English History from the Earliest Times to about 1485.* 1915. The standard bibliographic source for material in English history before 1485. Continued period by period by the following:

Bibliography of British History: Tudor Period 1485-1603, Stuart Period 1603-1714. 1928, 1933. 2 vol. Classified, selective list of books, articles, pamphlets, and documents relative to the two periods. Author and subject index.

——: *the Eighteenth Century, 1714-1789.* 1951. Author, title, and subject indexes.

With Gross (above) these two works form a continuous bibliographic index of English history to 1789.

Grose, Clyde Leclare. *A Select Bibliography of British History, 1660-1760.* 1939. An annotated, classified list of books and manuscripts.

Williams, Judith B. *A Guide to the Printed Materials for English Social and Economic History, 1750-1850.* 1926. 2 vol. A classified index with alphabetical index.

Milne, A. T. *Writings on British History.* An annual list of works on British history published during the year. Subject division. Volumes in print cover the years 1934-1945.

History of England. 1904-1956. 8 vol. The volumes have

been frequently reissued and brought up to date. A standard, detailed history of England. Each volume contains a bibliography of sources. Each volume the work of an eminent historian.

Political History of England. 1905-1915. 12 vol. A standard history, each volume the work of one or two specialists in the period. Contains lists of bibliographic sources. A very useful work, now somewhat out of date.

Oxford History of England. 1939-1962 (in progress). Each volume the work of a specialist in the field. Extensive chronological treatment, with bibliography. An important source.

Low, Sidney and F. S. Pulling. *Dictionary of English History.* 1928. A concise one-volume dictionary with brief articles on persons, subjects, and events in English history. Contains a bibliographic reference for most articles.

Cheney, Christopher R. *Handbook of Dates for Students of Modern History.* 1945. A useful handbook of dates for persons and events that a student of English history might encounter.

Literature

As an aid in finding information in this section, literature has been divided into sections: classical literature (Greek and Roman), American literature, and English literature. English literature has been subdivided into Old and Middle English, Medieval, and Modern. In the section on English literature, general works that cover the entire range of English literature will be found before all other works.

CLASSICAL

Year's Work in Classical Studies. 1906-1947. An annual survey of the work done in classical literature. No longer published.

Harvey, Sir Paul. *Oxford Companion to Classical Literature.* 1940. A handbook to Greek and Roman writers, subjects, and forms. Short articles on all subjects. Alphabetical arrangement. Has a useful date chart to classical literature.

Oxford Classical Dictionary. 1949. A good, scholarly work with signed articles and bibliographies. Covers biography, philosophy, mythology, literature, etc.

The New Century Classical Handbook. ed. Catherine B. Avery. 1962. A general handbook to classical literature. Short articles on all subjects of interest to the student.

Peck, Harry T. *Harper's Dictionary of Classical Literature and Antiquities.* 1897. A generally useful work covering the general field of Greek and Roman literature. Signed articles and bibliographies.

Sandys, Sir John Edwin. *Companion to Latin Studies.* 1929. Articles by specialists on subjects of interest in literature and history. Covers the various phases of Latin civilization. Useful to supplement the classical dictionary. Bibliographies.

Whibley, Leonard. *Companion to Greek Studies.* 1931. Similar in scope and intention to Sandys, above. Bibliographies.

Harsh, Philip Whaley. *A Handbook of Classical Drama.* 1944. Discusses Greek and Roman dramatists and their plays. Very useful annotated bibliographies that often suggest translations and editions for students.

AMERICAN

Leary, Lewis G. *Articles on American Literature,* 1900-1950. A subject list of articles on American literature appearing in a broad group of American and British periodicals. Three-quarters of the work is devoted to alphabetical articles on individual authors. There is also a subject list that groups articles under such titles as "Frontier and Foreign Influence," etc. A very useful bibliography. Continued by the annual bibliography published as the March supplement to the *Publications* of the Modern Language Association.

Blanck, Jacob. *Bibliography of American Literature.* 1955-1963 (in progress). A selective bibliography of American literature that will include, when complete, the work published in book form of about 300 authors, as well as selected list of bibliographic, biographic, and critical works about the author. When it is completed, it will be the standard bibliographic tool.

Cambridge History of American Literature. 1917-1921. 3 vol. The standard history for many years, and still one of the most important. Written by specialists. Author, title, and subject index to each volume.

Literary History of the United States. 1960. The first comprehensive history of American literature since the *Cambridge History.* The standard one-volume history. Articles on authors, periods, movements, etc. Part two is a selective bibliographic list of works in the essay form. Section four of the bibliography deals with individual authors, and lists the standard works and editions, bibliographies, biographies, and critical studies. This section is very useful.

Hart, James David. *The Oxford Companion to American Literature.* 1956. An alphabetical handbook that includes biography, style, subject matter, plot summaries, and other related matters of American authors. Contains selected bibliographies of the authors' works. Contains a useful chronological index to American literature.

Burke, William J. and Will D. Howe. *American Authors and Books, 1640-1940.* 1962. Similar to the *Oxford Companion* (above), but the articles are shorter and the coverage greater.

Kunitz, Stanley J. and Howard Haycraft. *American Authors, 1600-1900.* 1938. Short biographical sketches, with brief bibliographies of works by and about the author.

ENGLISH

General

Cambridge Bibliography of English Literature. 1941-1957. The most comprehensive and important bibliography in English literature. Arranged chronologically and by literary form. Volume four is an index to the first three volumes; volume five is a supplement that extends the bibliography from 1900 to 1955. For each author treated, gives the standard collected and separate works, selected bibliographic, biographic, and critical studies.

Watson, George, *Concise Cambridge Bibliography of English Literature, 1600-1950*. A selection of about 400 authors from the *C.B.E.L.* For each list, works both by and about. Includes a section that brings the *C.B.E.L.* up to 1950.

Northrup, Clark S. *A Register of Bibliographies of the English Language and Literature*. 1925. A useful list of bibliographies, both separately published and included in other works, of periods, movements, trends, authors, etc., in one alphabetical list.

Van Patten, Nathan. *Index to Bibliographies . . . 1923-1932*. Continues Northrup's *Register*, but lists only works about authors, British and American.

Modern Humanities Research Association. *Annual Bibliography of English Language and Literature*. 1921-present. An annual bibliography of English and American language and literature.

Year's Work in English Studies. 1919/20-present. An annual survey by period of the important work in the field; covers the same area as the *Annual Bibliography*, above, but is more fully annotated.

Cambridge History of English Literature. 1907-1927. The most complete and important history of English literature. Each chapter is by a specialist, and the bibliographies are extensive.

Oxford History of English Literature. 1945-(in progress). Unlike the *Cambridge History*, each volume of the *Oxford History* is the work of one outstanding scholar. The treatment of the period is therefore more uniform. The bibliographies are extensive.

A Literary History of England. 1948. An excellent one-volume history of English literature. Each section written by a specialist. Treats both individual authors and literary forms. Good, selected bibliographies.

Allibone, Samuel. *Critical Dictionary of English Literature*. 1858-1891. A standard work that contains a vast amount of biographical information (46,000 author entries) and some discussion of subject material. Although out of date, Allibone is still very useful for English literature up to the latter half of the nineteenth century. Supplement in 2 vol. by John Foster Kirk, 1892.

Chambers' Cyclopaedia of English Literature. 1938. A chronological encyclopedia that contains a large number of biographical sketches and some treatment of literary forms and subjects. Signed articles, with a general author and title index in the third volume.

Harvey, Paul. *Oxford Companion to English Literature.* 1946. A useful one-volume dictionary of authors, forms, works, characters in works, etc.

Briscoe, John D. and others. *A Mapbook of English Literature.* 1936. Literary and historical maps of England and some of the major cities, the Lake Country, etc.

Goode, Clement T. and E. F. Shannon. *An Atlas of English Literature.* 1925. By period, with London, Ireland and Scotland treated separately.

Old English and Middle English

Wells, John Edwin. *Manual of the Writings in Middle English, 1050-1400.* An important handbook to the literature up to 1400. Gives for each work listed the probable date, the MS or MSS, the dialect, and bibliography. Abstracts some of the longer works and contains some critical discussion. Ninth Supplement, 1961.

Loomis, Roger Sherman. *Introduction to Medieval Literature, Chiefly in England.* A selected reading list and bibliography. Emphasis on Celtic and English.

1400-1700

Hazlitt, William Carew. *Handbook to the Popular, Poetical, and Dramatic Literature of Great Britain.* 1867.

——. *Bibliographical Collections and Notes on Early English Literature, 1474-1700.*

Gray, G. J. *General Index to Hazlitt's Handbook and His Bibliographical Collections.* An important handbook and bibliographical index to the period.

Tannenbaum, Samuel A. and Dorothy R. Tannenbaum. *Elizabethan Bibliographies*. 1937-1947. A collection of about forty individual bibliographies of the major Elizabethan figures; there are individual bibliographies for many plays by Shakespeare.

1600-present

Crane, Ronald S. and Louis I. Bredvold. *English Literature, 1660-1800*. A bibliography of modern studies, comprising the annual bibliographies published in the *Philosophical Quarterly* from 1926-1960. Lists both the name of the author and of the subject of the study; includes selected topic entries.

Bernbaum, Ernest. *Guide Through the Romantic Movement*. 1949. Treats the chief figures, and includes concise, selected bibliographies. A valuable handbook for the period.

Ehrsham, Theodore G., Robert Deily, and Robert Smith. *Twelve Victorian Bibliographies*. 1936. Selected bibliographies of the major Victorian writers.

Bibliographies of Studies in Victorian Literature, ed. Austin Wright. A year-by-year (1945-1954) annotated listing of the scholarly work in Victorian literature.

Millett, Fred B. *Contemporary British Literature*. 1935. A critical survey that includes 232 author bibliographies.

Tindall, William York. *Forces in Modern British Literature, 1855-1956*. A general survey of the period, with brief bibliographical references.

Kunitz, Stanley J. and Howard Haycraft. *Twentieth Century Authors*. 1942. A biographical dictionary that includes bibliographies by and about the authors.

No biographical dictionaries have been listed for any period other than the modern, because the more general biographical dictionaries normally include any deceased author of note.

In addition to these general works, students should be aware of the extensive material normally available about every major author: biographies, bibliographies, critical studies, and concordances. None of these are listed in this work, because the card catalogue and the reference works in this section serve as indexes to these works.

Philosophy

Rand, Benjamin. *Bibliography of Philosophy, Psychology, and Cognate Subjects.* 1949. 2 vol. The most important bibliography of philosophy available. Forms volume 3 of Baldwin, *Dictionary of Philosophy*, listed below. The bibliography records works up to 1900. Now unfortunately out of date, but still useful. Deals with topics and authors.

Bibliography of Philosophy, 1933-1936. vol. 1-4. Reprinted from the *Journal of Philosophy*. A classified list of all the important philosophical works published during these years in English, French, German, and Italian.

Baldwin, James Mark. *Dictionary of Philosophy and Psychology.* 1901-1905. 3 vol. in 4. Reprinted 1940-49. Short, precise articles on all aspects of the field; signed articles by specialists. Most articles have bibliographies. While this work is out of date for more recent developments, it is an authoritative source for what it covers. Contains biographies of important individuals who were deceased when the work was written.

Who's Who in Philosophy. 1942. Contains biographical and bibliographical information about noted living philosophers. Short articles arranged alphabetically.

Runes, Dagobert D. *A Dictionary of Philosophy.* Concise, signed articles by specialists.

Philosophic Abstracts. Index. Vol. 1-16. An index to philosophical literature for the period 1939-1954. Arranged by country. Alphabetical within country.

Psychology

Chandler, Albert and E. N. Barnhart. *A Bibliography of Psychological and Experimental Aesthetics*, 1864-1937. 1938. Lists books and periodicals in the field, from 1865 to 1937. Divided into subject fields.

Harvard University. Departments of Psychology and Social Relations. *The Harvard List of Books in Psychology.* 1949, supplement 1958. An annotated bibliography of more than 600 important books, arranged by class, with author indexes.

Psychological Abstracts. 1927-present. A monthly abstract of books and articles by subject. Author and subject index. Abstracts are signed. A very important tool in this field.

Psychological Index, 1894-1935. 42 vol. An annual classified bibliography of all original publications in consciousness and behavior. Lists author and title of about 5000 works a year. Discontinued—continued by *Psychological Abstracts,* above.

Psychological Index. *Abstract References.* 1940-1941. 2 vol. Compiled to serve as a backward extension of *Psychological Abstracts.* Must be used in conjunction with the *Psychological Index,* as the periodicals are listed by the number found in the *Index.*

Annual Review of Psychology. 1950-present. An annual review of works published in the field. Divided into subject areas, each subject has an essay devoted to recent developments in the field. A valuable work for recent developments.

Grinstein, Alexander. *The Index of Psychoanalytic Writings.* 1956-1958. vol. 1-4. (In progress.) Lists books, articles, reviews, and abstracts, published by persons of note in psychoanalysis. Subject index announced.

Mental Health Book Review Index. 1956-present. Semiannual. The *Index* lists a review if it appears in three or more of the 96 journals covered. Includes psychology, psychiatry, and psychoanalysis.

English, Horace and Ava English. *A Comprehensive Dictionary of Psychological and Psychoanalytic Terms.* 1958. An excellent alphabetical dictionary of terms in use in both fields.

Drever, James. *A Dictionary of Psychology.* 1952. A good, small, inexpensive dictionary. Short, often one-line, definitions.

Psychological Register. 1929-32. vol. 2-3. Short biographical sketches and extensive bibliographies for psychologists throughout the world, arranged by country. Volume one has not yet appeared. Very much out of date.

Religion

Encyclopedia of Religion and Ethics. 1908-1927. 12 vol. and index. Revised 1951. The most comprehensive work on the subject. Signed articles by specialists, with full bibliographies. Somewhat out of date for recent developments.

Schaff, Philip. *New Schaff-Herzog Encyclopedia of Religious Knowledge.* 1908-1912. 12 vol. and index. One of the most important encyclopedias in the field. Very comprehensive, with full bibliographies. Extensive biographies, including biographies of men living at the time the work was published.

Twentieth Century Encyclopedia of Religious Knowledge. 1955. 2 vol. A supplement to the Schaff-Herzog, above. Signed articles with bibliographies. Includes biographies of people living and dead. Brings articles in the earlier work up to date, and includes some subjects not treated before.

Ferm, Vergilius. *An Encyclopedia of Religion.* A good one-volume work that covers the entire field. Includes biographies and bibliography.

Allison, William Henry. *History of Christianity.* 1931. An annotated bibliography of works on the history of Christianity and the church.

Case, Shirley J. *Bibliographical Guide to the History of Christianity.* 1931. A selected annotated guide to the literature of the history of Christianity. Divided into subjects, with an author and subject index.

Smith, William and Samuel Cheetham. *Dictionary of Christian Antiquities.* 1875-1880. 2 vol. Treats all subjects connected with the church except literature, sects, doctrines, etc., covered by the companion volume listed below. Long, signed articles with bibliographies. Out of date, but still useful.

Smith, William and Henry Wace. *Dictionary of Christian Biography, Literature, Sects, and Doctrine.* 1877-1887. 4 vol. Treats the subject from the time of the Apostles to the age of Charlemagne (approximately the year 800). Signed articles with bibliographies.

Wace, Henry and William Piercy. 1911. *A Dictionary of Christian Biography and Literature.* A revised and abridged version of Smith's *Dictionary of Christian Biography,* above.

Catholic Encyclopedia. 1907-1922. 17 vol. The standard work in this field. Long, signed articles by specialists, with good bibliographies.

Universal Jewish Encyclopedia. 1939-1944. 10 vol. The most up-to-date work in the field. Some articles are signed, and some contain bibliographies. The work treats all aspects of the field, including biography.

Mythology of All Races. 1916-1932. 13 vol., with index. The most important reference work in the field in English. Treats all races and all periods. Divided into broad subject areas, each written by a scholar in the field.

Frazer, James George. *The Golden Bough.* 1907-1915. 12 vol. and supplement (1936). An outstanding work on primitive religious beliefs.

Funk and Wagnalls Dictionary of Folklore, Mythology and Legend. 1949-1950. A worthwhile two-volume work. Some articles are signed, and some have bibliographies.

Sociology

Encyclopedia of the Social Sciences. 1930-1935. 15 vol. Covers all important topics in sociology, psychology, political science, anthropology, etc. Signed articles by specialists, many with extensive bibliographies. A large amount of biography. The most generally useful work in the social sciences. Reissued 1951-1957.

Public Affairs Information Service. *Bulletin.* 1915-present. A weekly index that cumulates five times a year, the last cumulation forming the annual index. A current index to economics, political science, government, sociology, etc. Subject index.

London Bibliography of the Social Sciences. 1931-1960. A subject bibliography that lists in all a million items. Alphabetical arrangement by subject. 4 vol. and 2 supplements; 5th vol. new index complete to 1960.

Dictionary of Sociology, ed. Henry Pratt Fairchild. 1944. Brief signed articles defining sociological terms. Sociology is defined rather widely, so some terms from anthropology, psychology, and related fields are included.

Current Sociology. 1952-present. Three issues yearly. An international index to sociological literature. In general, each issue deals with a different aspect of the field (i.e., sociology of marriage); therefore all issues should be checked.

International Bibliography of Sociology. 1952-present. An annual index to the literature on the subject. Indexes over 500 periodicals, by subject field. Subject and author index to the classified listings. A very important tool.

Sociological Abstracts. Nov. 1952-date. Abstracts articles of interest to the field. Divided into broad subject fields.

CHAPTER 10

A SAMPLE RESEARCH PAPER

The following literary research paper originally appeared in *The New York Public Library Bulletin,* November 1960. The notes in the left margin indicate standard research writing techniques exemplified in the paper.

*sample
title
page*

```
        The Reception of Synge's Playboy in
          Ireland and America: 1907-1912




                      Student's Name_____

                      Class         _____

                      Date          _____

                      Instructor's Name_____
```

THE RECEPTION OF SYNGE'S <u>PLAYBOY</u> IN

IRELAND AND AMERICA: 1907-1912

by Daniel J. Murphy

note that the title introduces the topic

general introduction—gets the reader to the subject and tells him the topic of the paper

A few years ago in New York, John
Millington Synge's <u>The</u> <u>Playboy</u> <u>of</u> <u>the</u>
<u>Western</u> <u>World,</u> one of the most famous
plays of the Irish literary renaissance,
had a very successful and profitable
two-year run in an off-Broadway theatre.
One would have thought, from the ease
of the players on the stage, the re-
laxation and delight of the audience,
and the lack of any police protection,
that it was always thus with Synge's
play. However, the reception of <u>The</u>
<u>Playboy</u> today contrasts noticeably
with the reception of the play by
Synge's contemporaries. Most Irishmen—
in both Ireland and America—objected to
the play's production, and riots occurred in Dublin in 1907 and in America
in 1911. To understand this antagonism

theme statement

to Synge's masterpiece it is necessary
to comprehend the political situation
in Ireland and the situation of the
American Irish at the turn of the
century. It was a time of turmoil for
the Irish at home, and transition for

the Irish abroad.

In Ireland the sensational divorce
case of Kitty O'Shea, instituted in
December 1889, in which Charles Stewart

Parnell, Irish nationalist leader, was
named corespondent, deposed Parnell
as the leader of the Irish nationalist
movement, and split Irish nationalists
into Parnellite and anti-Parnellite.
Healing this split in the political
movement for Home Rule was a long and
bitter process; politically Ireland
remained divided for years.[1] Some repair
in the cleavage was achieved, however,
from a movement which was initially
non-political and hence able to unite
Irish energies in an Irish cause.
Douglas Hyde, speaking to the Irish

---

[1] In the Preface to Parnell and his Party
(Oxford, 1957) Conor Cruise O'Brien
writes: "to this day in Ireland,
certain families are apt to regard each
other with an animosity derived from the
events of 1890 and fading only slowly from
generation to generation. Few blood-
less struggles in modern times can
have produced such intense and lasting
loyalties and resentments as did the
crisis over the leadership of the Irish
party and people after the verdict in
the divorce case, O'Shea v O'Shea
and Parnell."
   A vivid artistic description of the
controversy can be read in Chapter 1 of
James Joyce's A Portrait of the Artist
as a Young Man.

Literary Society of Dublin in support

of the Gaelic League, November 25, 1892,

delivered a lecture entitled The Neces-

sity for de-Anglicizing Ireland:

full colon to introduce direct quotation

direct quotation indented and single-spaced; no quote marks

> When we speak of "The Necessity for
> de-Anglicizing the Irish Nation,"
> we mean it, not as a protest against
> imitating what is best in the Eng-
> lish people, for that would be
> absurd, but rather to show the folly
> of neglecting what is Irish, and
> hastening to adopt, pell-mell, and
> indiscriminately, everything that
> is English, simply because it is
> English. . . . In a word, we
> must strive to cultivate every-
> thing that is most racial,
> most smacking of the soil,
> most Gaelic, most Irish,
> because in spite of the little
> admixture of Saxon blood in the
> north east corner, this island is
> and will ever remain Celtic to the
> core. . . . We must create a strong
> feeling against West Britonism, for
> it—if we give it the least chance,
> or show it the smallest quarter—
> will overwhelm us like a flood,
> and we shall find ourselves toiling
> painfully behind the English at
> each step, following the same
> fashions, only six months behind the
> English ones; reading the same
> books, only months behind them;
> taking up the same fads, after they
> have become stale there, following
> them in our dress, literature, music,
> games, and ideas, only a long time
> after them and a vast way behind.[2]

transitional phrase and topic sentence

Some six years after this speech

D. P. Moran published in The New Ireland

Review, between 1898 and 1900, a series

---

[2]Revival of Irish Literature, ad-
dresses by Sir Charles Gavan Duffy,
Dr. George Sigerson and Dr. Douglas Hyde
(London, 1894), pp. 117-118.

of six articles in which he militantly
theorized that the nation was dying
at the roots, but could be saved by concentrating on the essentials of
nationality. The articles constituted
a potent, detailed, and aggressive
restatement of Dr. Hyde's thesis on the
necessity of de-Anglicizing Ireland.
The articles would not, however, have
influenced Irish opinion had not the
author, in 1900, founded a weekly newspaper, The Leader to explain and
popularize the philosophy of Irish-
Ireland. In 1905, when The Leader was
popular, Moran reprinted the articles,
which, he said, "contain the reflec-
tions, the arguments, and register the
convictions that led up to the starting
of The Leader." Moran argued that
the Protestant Parliament, and the
non-Gael generally, were not Irish at
all, but simply "English who happened
to be born in Ireland."ª Moran was
not alone in emphasizing the basic
cleavage in the Irish nation. Dr.
Mahaffy, Provost of Trinity College,

Marginal notes:
- articles para-phrased because direct quotation would be too lengthy
- quotation con-tained in text because less than 5 lines
- paraphrase and direct quotation
- standard foot-note form— footnotes are numbered consecutively

---

ªP. S. O'Hegarty, A History of Ireland
Under the Union, 1801-1922 (London,
1952), p. 623.

noted that Catholic and Protestant were
once more ranged against each other,

paraphrase and
direct quotation

making "the contest not only of two
creeds, but two breeds, two ways of
thinking, of two ways of looking at all
the most vital interests of men."[4]

transition by
repetition of key
word "Moran"

Moran's articles had an effect on
the popular conception of what constituted Irish literature. Yeats, Synge,
Lady Gregory, AE, and others were
Anglo-Irish, were writing in English, and
consequently this literature was scrut-
inized closely by both the nationalist
and Gaelic Leaguer. According
to the new Catholic generation,
they did not have sufficient
sympathy, writes John Eglinton, "for
such movements as that for the revival
of the Irish language, or for the
political program of Sinn Fein. . . .
There was always something uncongenial
to Catholic Ireland in Anglo-Irish
literature: it galled the Catholic
youth to be a subject race, subject not
only politically but in a literary sense.
They wanted a literature and a nationality which they could call their

[4] W. Alison Phillips, Revolution in Ireland, 1906-1923 (New York, 1923), p, 52.

direct quotation
own. . . ."⁵ When Anglo-Irish literature
was not antithetical to the aims of the
Gaelic League and the Irish Nationalists, there was little overt
opposition; some plays, like Yeats's
Cathleen ni Houlihan, were even considered Irish and Nationalist. However,
besides such plays were others which
disturbed Irish Catholic sensitivity,
and when, in 1899, at the very beginning
of the Irish Literary Theatre, Yeats's
The Countess Cathleen was performed
at the Antient Concert Rooms, there
was opposition by Catholics who thought
the play an "insult to their faith."⁶
Much of the opposition came from a

citation in text
pamphlet, "Souls for Gold," by F. Hugh
O'Donnell, which had been widely distributed before the performance.

series of parallel
phrases—inter-
nally punctuated
and separated
by semicolons
O'Donnell resented the play's pagan,
anti-Catholic attitude; resented Yeats's
thesis that the Countess, who had
sold her soul for gold, would never-

---

⁵William K. Magee, Irish Literary Portraits (London, 1935), p. 27. John Eglinton was the pseudonym of W. K. Magee. He
was for some time Assistant Director of
the National Library of Ireland.

⁶Lady Isabelle Augusta Gregory, Our Irish
Theatre (New York, 1913), pp. 23-24.

theless go to Heaven; objected to many of the characters in the drama; and blasted the supposition that Irish peasants would sell their souls for gold, a criticism of the play that had widespread support in the press. The play was hissed and booed so vigorously that the police were called, for an attack on the actors was feared. Yeats's play was denounced by the Dublin Catholic students; Cardinal Logue, asked to comment, wrote:

full colon to introduce a lengthy direct quotation— indented and single-spaced.

> All I know of this play is what I could gather from the extracts given in Mr. O'Donnell's pamphlet and your paper. Judging by these extracts, I have no hesitation in saying that an Irish-Catholic audience which could patiently sit out such a play must have sadly degenerated, both in religion and patriotism.[7]

transition by repetition of key phrase

The criticism of <u>The Countess Cathleen</u> affected the reputation of Yeats and those associated with him, and impugned the nationalistic intentions of the Irish Literary Theatre. In

paraphrase

a letter to Lady Gregory, Yeats says that Bullen, trying to sell his books in Dublin, encountered great hostility among the booksellers. They regarded

---

[7]Lennox Robinson, <u>Ireland's Abbey Theatre</u> (London, 1951), p. 6.

Yeats as heterodox. George Russell (AE)
told Yeats that clerical influence—
Father Finlay and his Jesuits—was
working with Moran. Yeats felt that
the <u>Countess</u> <u>Cathleen</u> dispute accounted
for a good deal of this antagonism.*
The dispute arose, Yeats believed,

direct quotation because "in using what I considered
traditional symbols, I forgot that in
Ireland they are not symbols but
realities. But the attack in the main . . .
came from the public ignorance of

footnoted in the text since it was convenient to do so at the end of the paragraph literary method" (W. B. Yeats,
<u>Dramatis</u> <u>Personae</u> [New York, 1936]
pp. 326-37).

transition by repetition of key phrases   The conflict between symbol and
reality; between literary method and

parallel structure the public conception of it; between
the nationalistic Irish-Irish and the
universality of artistic theme and
involvement, soon plunged the Abbey
into another dispute. Synge's <u>In</u> <u>the</u>
<u>Shadow</u> <u>of</u> <u>the</u> <u>Glen</u> was considered

direct quotation un-Irish. "Who was John Synge?" the
public demanded. "He was Anglo-Irish—
that was certain; he was of the land-

---

*<u>Letters</u> <u>of</u> <u>W.</u> <u>B.</u> <u>Yeats</u>, ed. Allen Wade
(New York, 1954), p. 350.

owning class, the class that raked all
that muck about Ireland into English
journals and into religio-politico
publications." Moreover, he was attacking the virtue of Irish women, and
that was what distinguished Ireland

*footnote at end
of paraphrase
following direct
quote*

from the de-civilized lands to the east
of her.[9]

Arthur Griffith's <u>The United</u>

<u>Irishman</u>, a nationalist paper and

*reference worked
into text*

the forerunner of <u>Sinn Fein</u>, attacked
the play (Oct. 17, 1903). Griffith
argued that Synge's play had nothing
Irish about it, that it was more characteristic of Continental decadent
literature than of Irish:

> The play is a staging of a corrupt
> version of that old-world libel on
> womankind—the Widow of Ephesus. . . .
> Men and women in rural Ireland,
> according to Mr. Synge, marry lacking
> love, and as a consequence, this
> woman proves un-faithful. Mr. Synge
> never found that in Irish life. Men
> and women in Ireland marry lacking
> love, and live mostly in a dull level
> of amity. . . .
> Mr. Synge . . . places Nora Burke
> before us as a type—a personifica-
> tion of an average—and Nora Burke
> is a lie. It is not by staging a
> lie we can serve Ireland or
> exalt Art.

After attacking Synge's play,

---

[9] Padraic Colum, <u>Road Round Ireland</u> (New
York, 1937), p. 360.

Griffith attacked Yeats for stating
that art must integrate nationalism
into art if nationalism is to use art
at all: "Mr. Yeats writes that the
Irish National Theatre Society has no
propaganda but that of good art. If so,
the society is no more Irish and National
than the Elizabethan Stage Society."
If the theatre ceases to be nationalistic, continues the article, "it will
also cease to be artistic, for nationality is the breath of art."

Responding to Yeats's appeal for the
freedom of the artist, Maude Gonne
called for freedom from "the insidious
and destructive tyranny of foreign

reference in text   influence" (<u>United Irishman</u>, Oct. 24,
1903). This Irish-Irish attitude was
amplified by another correspondent in
the same issue of the <u>United Irishman</u>:
"If the spirit of nationalism were free
and untrammeled, and had not to fight
for existence and recognition; if she
could afford to assimilate foreign
ideas without detriment to her own
vitality, the artist could have complete

freedom."[10] Moran's The Leader commented that Synge saw only the worst
side of Irish life, and presented that
side exclusively; that Synge showed
Nora Burke, the heroine, behaving in
an objectionable manner while her
supposedly dead husband was in the room.

Synge's The Well of the Saints,
performed less than two years later,
did little to allay Irish suspicions
that his motives and methods were foreign
and decadent. Joseph Holloway, whose
diary is invaluable for this period,
reports that several members of the
National Literary Society felt the play
low, vulgar, and extremely degrading
to the Irish. The play, which Holloway
had seen in rehearsal, reminded him
of a slang dictionary, with its brutal,
coarse language and its insult to the
Catholic Church. He felt its performance
would ruin the Abbey. One of the actresses, Miss Garvey, told Holloway
she had refused to appear in the play

---

explanatory
footnote—
notice the short
form used for
second citation
of Yeats's
Letters

[10] Yeats considered challenging Griffith
to a public debate over "our two poli-
cies—his that literature should be
subordinate to nationalism, and mine
that it should have its own ideal"
(Letters, pp. 421-422).

until some alterations were made in
the language. The play was not a success.
Only fifty people were in the theater
for the third performance.[11]

Opposition to the theater continued.
In the latter part of 1905 and the early
part of 1906, several members left the
Abbey because of dissension over politics, over roles, and over the payment
of actors. They felt the theater was
too commercial, and was divorcing itself
from the national government. The group
formed a rival, nationalistically
oriented company. Padraic Colum, Catholic and a nationalist, whose play,
Broken Soil, had been an Abbey success
in December 1903, gave his play The
Land to the new company. In addition,
dissension continued among the actors
who remained. One of the company wrote
to The United Irishman (March 1906)
repeating the charge that the National
Theatre Society was artistic rather
than nationalistic. Yeats was accused
of foisting a literary movement on the

---

[11] Joseph Holloway, "A Dublin Playgoer's
Impression" (1905), pp. 16, 20, 47, 72.
These unpublished MS diaries are in
the National Library, Dublin.

Irish people as a national movement, and accused of artistic rather than nationalistic aims. It was at this period, January 1907, when the Abbey was recovering from these controversies, that Synge's <u>The Playboy of the Western World</u> was put into rehearsal.

Dublin was filled with rumors about the new play. Mary Colum wrote that during the rehearsal period reports spread through Dublin that the play contained improprieties, and that the womanhood of Ireland was being slandered.[12] The directors took extraordinary precautions during rehearsals to prevent outsiders from seeing the play. Joseph Holloway, who ordinarily had free access to the theater, was told by William Fay that there was a new rule that no one could be present at rehearsals (Holloway, Jan. 8, 1907, p. 19). Fay "gave <u>The Playboy</u> long and careful rehearsal, doing my best to tone down the bitterness of it, and all the time with a sinking heart. I knew we were in for trouble, but

long form for first citation— if a second citation were used it would simply be Mary Colum, p.—

---

[12] Mary Colum, <u>Life and the Dream</u> (New York, 1947), p. 137.

it was my business to get Synge's play
produced as nearly to his notions as
possible in the circumstances and with
the material at my disposal."[13]

When Lady Gregory came from Gort to
Dublin on Saturday, January 26, a note
from Synge awaited her: "I do not
know how things will go tonight. The
day company are all very steady but
some of the outsiders are in a deplorable
state of uncertainty."[14] Both Willy
and Frank Fay told Holloway that they
expected trouble with the audience
(Holloway, Jan. 1907, p. 66).

The first night audience was larger
than usual, and there was a great deal
of expectancy and tenseness. The first
act was well received, the audience
enjoying the humor. The second act was
received less enthusiastically, but
was also applauded, even if the audience
appeared somewhat shocked and puzzled
at the wild language. At the conclusion
of the second act, Lady Gregory sent a
telegram to Yeats, who was lecturing

---

[13] W. G. Fay and Catherine Carswell, _Fays
of the Abbey Theatre_ (London, 1935), p.
213.

short form after
first citation   [14] Lady Gregory, p. 131.

in Scotland: "Play great success."
The telegram was, however, premature;
the audience's uneasiness during the
second act was evidently repressed
hostility, for in the middle of the third
act the audience exploded into a
hissing, shouting mob at the point where
Christy says to the Widow Quin:

> It's Pegeen I'm seeking only, and
> what'd I care if you brought me a
> drift of chosen females, standing
> in their shifts itself, maybe, from
> this place to the Eastern World?

Not a word was audible from this
speech to the play's conclusion. A new
telegram was sent to Yeats: "Audience

citation in text—
notice short form
used for citation
of Lady
Gregory's *Our
Irish Theatre.*

broke up in disorder at the word shift"
(Lady Gregory, p. 112). As Lady Gregory
left the theater she met Joseph Holloway
and asked him what he thought was the
cause of the disturbance. "Black-
guardism," was his answer. When she
asked him on which side, Holloway
answered pat, "The Stage!" (Holloway,
Jan. 1907, p. 63). Many of Holloway's
friends objected to the play; MacNamara,
a fellow architect, told him he was
delighted he had not taken his wife;
he had never been so taken aback in his
life, and had hissed for all he was

worth. Another friend said Synge's mind
needed a sanitary inspector to look
after it; and Moran, editor of The Leader,
had refused to take his wife, fearing
what she might hear from the stage.

The audience, perhaps, would not
have objected so violently to words such
as "bloody" and "shift" had not
Synge, in the preface to the Program
claimed realism for the language. All
the words used in the play were "heard
among the country people of Ireland, or
spoken in my own nursery before I could
read the newspapers." On the stage,
wrote Synge, one must have reality.
It was this claim for realism that
antagonized the audience; they could
not believe that Irish women would run
after a parricide, or that realism could
be claimed for the language.

direct quotation
and paraphrase

Newspaper comments on the play were
generally antagonistic; one of the more
violent reviews was in the Freeman's
Journal, Jan. 28, 1907:

citation in text

> A strong protest must, however, be
> entered against this unmitigated,
> protracted libel upon Irish peasant
> men, and worse still, upon Irish
> peasant girlhood. The blood boils
> with indignation as one recalls the
> incidents, expressions, ideas of this

squalid, offensive production. . . .
No adequate idea can be given of
the barbarous jargon, the elaborate
and incessant cursing of these
repulsive creatures.

The _Irish_ _Independent_ objected to
the frequent use of "bloody" and
"damn." The _Irish_ _Times_ notice was
conservative, commenting that while
some expressions might be realistic and
taken from life, it was another thing
to put them on the stage in a huge city.
There was a great outcry that the play
be withdrawn.

transition and
topic sentence

In spite of the opposition, the
directors refused to withdraw the play.
Lady Gregory, in an interview with a
Freeman's _Journal_ reporter, stated:
"We have already declared publicly
that, in the opinion of those conducting
the theater, it is the fiddler who
chooses the tune. The public are quite
at liberty to stay away, but if they
come they must take what is provided for
them." She emphasized that _The_ _Playboy_
would be produced at the Abbey every night
during the week, as originally
scheduled.

As no performances were given on
Sunday, Synge's _Riders_ _to_ _the_ _Sea_ and

The Playboy were staged the Monday

following. Lady Gregory writes that

Riders to the Sea went very well indeed;

however, the atmosphere changed after

the curtain fell:

direct quotation
used freely here
to allow first-
hand witnesses
to describe the
scene—these
three lengthy
quotes are good
examples of the
use of primary
sources

> In the interval after it, I noticed
> on one side of the pit a large group
> of men sitting together, not a woman
> among them. I told Synge I thought
> it a sign of some organised dis-
> turbance and he telephoned to have
> the police at hand. The first part
> of the act went undisturbed. Then
> suddenly an uproar began. The group
> of men I had noticed booed, hooted,
> blew tin trumpets. . . . It was im-
> possible to hear a word of the play.
> The curtain came down for a minute,
> but I went round and told the actors
> to go on playing to the end, even if
> not a word could be heard. The police,
> hearing the uproar, began to file
> in, but I thought the disturbers
> might tire themselves out if left
> alone, or be satisfied with having
> made their protest, and I asked them
> to go outside but stay within call
> in case of any attempt being made
> to injure the players or the
> stage. . . . The disturbance lasted
> to the end of the evening, not one
> word having been heard after the
> first ten minutes. (Lady Gregory
> p. 112)
>
> At the end of the first act
> Mr. W. G. Fay came to the footlights
> and announced that it was the opinion
> of those concerned in the production
> of the comedy that anyone who did
> not like it would be well advised
> to leave the building. A crash of
> disorder was the response, and the
> lusty singing of "The West's
> asleep" followed in the interval
> before the curtain was raised
> again. . . . The final act was
> played amid cries of "Sinn Fein,"
> "Sinn Fein Amhain," and "Kill
> the author." (Robinson, pp. 53-54.)

Holloway, who attended every per-

formance during the week commented:

> The performance was just con-
> cluding amid a terrific roar. . . .
> The curtains were drawn aside and
> W. G. Fay stood forward amid the din.
> After some minutes in a lull he said,
> "You who have hissed tonight will go
> away saying you have heard the play.
> But you haven't." "We heard it
> on Saturday," came from the back
> of the pit, and the hissing and the
> hooting was renewed. The scene
> which followed was indescribable.
> Those in the pit howled for the
> author, and he with Lady Gregory
> and others held animated conversation
> in the stalls. . . . Small knots
> of people argued the situation out
> anything but calmly and after about a
> quarter of an hour's clamour the
> audience dispersed hoarse. (Hol-
> loway, Jan. 1907, p. 69).

Holloway writes that Synge was

furious. He stood on the steps leading

to the stalls with his hands raised,

defying the occupants who stood shouting

and waving their fists at him. Some

of Synge's friends were trying to pull

him away, but he wouldn't move, even

though the pit howled and threatened.

Mrs. Martin, the charwoman of the

Abbey, yelled at Holloway, who was

standing by, "Take him away, they'll

murder him," and in her excitement

caught Synge by the coat tails, trying

to pull him out into the vestibule.

Holloway replied, "Never fear for him,

he's all right—he's able to look after
himself. They'll do him no bodily
hurt." Synge stood his ground while
the protestors started to file out of
the theater shouting, "Withdraw the
play. We'll never let it get a hearing
in Dublin." Synge finally allowed
himself to be moved away, "he
looking the picture of silent deter-
mination—suppressed passion shaking
his burly frame." (Holloway, July
1924, p. 37).

In a subsequent interview regarding
his intentions in writing Playboy,
Synge said that, as he knew Irish life
best, he made his methods Irish. In
response to the question whether he
was concerned about the reality of the
play and the reaction of the audience,
Synge replied, "Yes, and I don't care
a rap how the people take it. I never
bother whether my plots are typical
Irish or not; but my methods are
typical. . . . We shall go on with the
play to the very end, in spite of
all. . . . I don't care a rap."[15]

---

explanatory
footnote to
establish the
authority of
the source

[15] W. A. Henderson 181, clipped from The
Evening Mail. As manager of the Abbey,
Henderson maintained a newspaper scrap-
book of Abbey matters. His collections,
cited here, are now in the National Library, Dublin.

This interview, printed under the
heading, "I don't care a rap," was
very damaging, and Synge immediately
regretted his angry words. On January
30 he wrote a letter to the Irish Times:

> The Playboy of the Western World
> is not a play with a purpose in the
> modern sense of the word, but although
> parts of it are meant to be extrava-
> gant comedy, still a great deal is
> in it, and a great deal more that
> is behind it, is perfectly serious
> when looked at in a certain light.
> (Irish Times, Jan. 31, 1907).

chronological
order

Yeats returned from Scotland in
time for the Tuesday performance. Lady
Gregory had in the meantime given seats
to some Trinity students in order to
have a favorable claque. Holloway said

paraphrase of
primary sources

they were drinking and, before long,
fighting with the rest of the audience;
one of them had to be ejected by Synge.
Before the performance began, Yeats
made a speech in which he invited all
to a public discussion of the play
Monday next at the Abbey. As soon as
the play started, the disturbances
began. Yeats tried three times to talk
to the audience, and three separate
attempts were made to continue the play.
The Freeman's Journal (Jan. 30) de-
scribes the scene that followed:

the use of
contemporary
newspapers as
primary sources

> The players were standing in a group
> on the stage, evidently alarmed at
> the turn affairs were taking . . .
> and discussing the situation amongst
> themselves. . . . Synge, Yeats and
> Lady Gregory held a conference when
> it was evident that the pit would
> not permit the play to proceed. After
> a few moments Lady Gregory left the
> theatre, and re-appeared with the
> police. However, although the police
> ejected the disturbers, there was
> no time during the evening when an
> entire sentence from the play could
> be heard.

At the conclusion of the performance,
the Trinity students jumped to the
stage and sang the English national
anthem, and the audience sang something
of "home growth." The Trinity students
had to be forcibly ejected and marched
to the college under police protection
(Holloway, Jan. 1907, p. 71). One of
the ejected nationalists said, "the
Abbey is now dead and rotten as a National
Theatre. . . . After Tuesday it is
absolutely certain that the Abbey cannot
be accepted as an Irish National
Institution" (Freeman's Journal, Jan.
30, 1907).

The demonstrations on Monday and
Tuesday were perhaps the most violent
the company endured. Wednesday's
performance was, however, by no means
quiet:

Cat calls, strident bugle notes, and the fierce demonstrations added to the general din . . . . For fully five minutes not a word spoken on the stage could be heard . . . but from then to the end of the act the dialogue was not completely smothered. . . . The second act, however, was all uproar, and concluded among a hurricane of uproar. The interval between the acts was occupied by a fist fight in the vestibule, and the singing of "The Peeler and the Goat." The third act was unintelligible, played amid bugle calls, hisses, applause and boos. After the performance, the house had to be cleared by the police, and demonstrators marched, under police surveillance, through Abbey Street and O'Connell Street (Freeman's Journal, Jan. 31).

The reporter from the Independent thought the rioting less intense than previously; he saw a number of intelligent and critical persons in the stalls and balcony. Some portion of the play was heard. Lady Gregory said that if the reception of the play improved, it would come off Saturday, but if it did not, it would be played until it received a fair hearing (Irish Independent, Feb. 1, 1907).

On Thursday the play, protected by more than two hundred police who lined the walls and the aisles, was partially heard for the first time since the opening performance. There was only occasional booing, and only two ar-

rests. The audience left the building
in good order. On Friday, the reception
was again good, the audience hearing
almost the entire play. Yeats met
Holloway and asked him what he thought
of the play. Holloway growled that he
did not like it at all, and mentioned
the drunken Trinity students who had
attended Tuesday's performance. Yeats
replied: "There were plenty of drunken
men in the pit, and he preferred drunken
men who applauded in the right than
drunken men who hissed . . . in the
wrong" (Holloway, Jan. 1907, pp.
25, 79).

On Saturday, Holloway reported that
the police "were as thick as black-
berries in September, and a row of them
sat alone in the center of the pit as
well as lining all the walls and filling
the scene dock and laneway and streets
outside" (p. 79). The Evening Herald
reported the play had a fair hearing
for the first time since it was staged,
and the police were not needed.

On the Monday following the final
performance of The Playboy, Yeats
opened the theater for a discussion of

the play and the reason for the directors'
refusal to withdraw it. Lady Gregory
described the meeting in a letter to
Synge, who had not attended:

> The theater was crammed; all the
> stalls had been taken. . . . Before
> it began there was whistling etc. . . .
> Yeats's first speech was fairly well
> listened to, though there were boos
> and cries. . . . No one came to
> support us. Russell was in the gallery
> we heard afterwards but did not come
> forward to speak. Colum "had a
> rehearsal" and didn't speak or
> come. T. W. Russell didn't turn up.
> We had hardly anyone to speak on our
> side at all, but it didn't much
> matter for the disturbances were so
> great they wouldn't even let their
> own speakers be well heard. Lawrence
> was first to attack us, a very poor
> speech, his point that we should
> have taken the play off because the
> audience and papers didn't like it.
> . . . But he bored the audience. . . .
> Old Yeats made a very good speech
> and got at first a very good re-
> ception, though when he went up
> there were cries of "Kill your
> father," "Get a loy" etc. and
> at the end when he praised Synge
> he was booed. . . .
> Yeats when he rose for the last
> speech was booed but got a hearing at
> last and got out all he wanted to
> say. He spoke very well, but his
> voice rather cracked once or twice
> from screaming and from his sore
> throat. I was sorry while there
> that we had ever let such a set inside
> the theatre, but I am glad today,
> and I think it was spirited and
> showed we were not repenting or
> apologizing.[16]

In his speech Yeats stated that when

use of letter by
an observer as a
primary source—
note here, how-
ever, that the
author of the
article did not
see the actual
ms letter, but
depended on a
secondary source
for its authen-
ticity—this is
standard schol-
arly practice

note the non-
regular use of *f*
to indicate the
following page
(249).

---

[16] David Herbert Greene and Edward
Stephens, _J. M. Synge_, _1871-1909_ (New
York, 1959), p. 248f.

the national leadership passed from
the hands of a few central leaders into
the hands of hundreds of little clubs,
they made unworthy fights for worthy
causes. They demanded all things Irish—
everyone had to wear Irish cloth, speak
Irish, hold similar political opinions.
"It needs eloquence to persuade and
intelligence to expand, but the coarser
means come ready to every man's hand,
as ready as a stone or a stick, and
where these coarse means are all, there
is nothing but mob, and the commonest
idea most prospers and is most sought
after."[17] Yeats said young men and
women wished again for individual
sincerity. "We are beginning once
again to ask what man is, and to be
content to wait a little before we
go on to that further question: What
is a good Irishman? . . . Manhood is all
and the root of manhood is courage
and courtesy."[18] Lady Gregory, as a
result of her support of the play, was
boycotted by the Gort town council;

---

[17] The Arrow, No. 3.

[18] W. B. Yeats, Plays and Controversies
(London, 1923), pp. 195-196.

they forbade the school children to
attend her teas and entertainments
lest their morals be corrupted.

conclusion of the
section dealing
with the Irish
reception, and
transition to the
section dealing
with the Ameri-
can reception.

Opposition to the aims of the theatre
and to Synge gradually diminished.
When The Playboy was revived in Dublin
on May 27, 1909, it was performed
without interruption. However, if the
Irish in Ireland were prepared to let
Synge lie peacefully in his grave, the
Irish in America were not. When the
Abbey took the company on its first
tour of America in 1911, it was necessary
to fight The Playboy battle all over
again.

Introduction of
new theme—and
the background
of cause of
American
reception

The causes for the American riots
over The Playboy were at once similar
to and different from those of the Dublin
riots. While it is true that the Irish
Nationalist movement in America was
extremely strong and culturally and
financially allied with the movement
in Ireland, so that it followed Dublin's
lead in denouncing Synge, the Irish-
Americans had another reason for ob-
jecting to The Playboy—they wished
to drive the Stage Irishman from the
theater. Irish-Americans reveled in
their Irish heritage, but they wished

to lose their identity as a minority
culture and be accepted as equals in
the culture in which they lived.

Every culture, when exposed to a new
mass immigration, uses stereotyped
conceptions by which the new group can
be most easily comprehended: witness
the stereotypes for Negroes, Germans,
Jews, and now Puerto-Ricans. At first,
unconscious of other implications, the
immigrant revels in the notoriety which
is fostered by the stage projections
of his most satirizable characteristics;
but as the immigrant becomes more con-
scious of the cultural role he is
committed to by these distortions, he
rebels. Art forms that repeat the
stereotype are protested; immigrants
who have obtained some stature in the
culture utilize media through which they
can protest the libel on their race
and through which they can project
different racial characteristics. The
Irish-American resented and objected
to such satirizations as the Stage
Irishman.

One of the first examples of the
Irish-American's reaction to the Stage

transition from
the generalized
cause to the
particular cause

specific example
to make the
general
particular

Irishman was the riot in New York over
the stage play McFadden's Row of Flats.
On March 19, 1903, two hundred Irishmen
attended the play's performance at the
New Star Theatre, each carrying four
eggs in his pockets and assorted vegetables under his hat. The men waited
until the principal actors were on the
stage, and then at a given signal
bombarded the actors with the eggs and
vegetables. The only principal actor
who didn't retreat to the wings was
the donkey (representing one of the
Irish traits), and he, faithful to his
own stereotype, resisted all attempts
to remove him from the barrage. One of
the actresses, Miss Inez Thomas, had
to use make-up to disguise the black
eye she had received from a flying egg
(New York Sun, Mar. 20).

There can be no doubt that this was
one outburst in an organized attempt
to suppress the Stage Irishman. Several
of those arrested said so, as did some
of those not arrested who talked to
reporters. Major Edward T. McCrystal,
one of the group's leaders, said to a
Sun reporter (Mar. 20): "The three

note again the
use of a news-
paper as a
primary source

great educators are the pulpit, the
press and the stage. Of the three where
liberty is most apt to degenerate into
license is the stage. It is indecent
to depict any race by exaggerating its
lowest feature, and to hold up to ridi-
cule an entire people because of any
poverty or faults of a small number."
Major McCrystal said the Stage Irishman
would be protested by the Clan-na Gael
and the Hibernians wherever he was found.

tying Ireland
and America
together

    The attempt to suppress the Stage
Irishman was not a temporary phenomenon.
Dudley Digges, Marie Quinn, and Gerald
Ewing, former Abbey actors, withdrew
from the cast of An Irishman's Stratagem
and AE's Deirdre as a protest over
performing on the same program with a
comedian portraying the Stage Irishman
at the St. Louis Exhibition (Gaelic
American, July 1904). John McCormack,
engaged to sing at the Exhibition,
refused to go on after a song that
depicted the St. Patrick's Day cele-
bration as one day's drunk and twenty-
nine days' recovery. McCormack said
the air was already disturbed because
of a performance on April 30, during

which the Irish were compared to monkeys.
When he was assured that such performances would not be repeated, he
returned for the remainder of his
contract.[19]

It was rather to be expected, therefore, that there would be opposition
to a play that the Dublin Irish had
denounced as an Anglo-Irish slur on
Irish womanhood and a travesty on
the Irish race. Having repeatedly
opposed the production of the Stage
Irishman, the American Irish would
naturally protest vehemently what
seemed to them the importation of one
from the mother country. The atmosphere
was certainly not propitious for the
production of The Playboy of the Western
World. American protests were destined
to be more vitriolic than had been the
Irish.

In September, 1911, before the Abbey
Players opened their American tour in
Boston, the Gaelic American, a paper of
extreme Irish sentiment, began attacking

---

[19] An interview in the St. Louis Evening
Mail, in Henderson I 262. The date was
probably some time in May (possibly the
24th), 1904.

some of the proposed plays, focusing
its attention on The Playboy. Its first
article (Sept. 10) claimed that the
Playboy lacked morality and proper
respect for the Irish people. Two weeks
later it reminded its readers that
The Playboy had been driven from the
Irish stage, and gave a most biased and
inaccurate synopsis of the play, which
fostered the impression that the play
was another representation of the
Stage Irishman (Sept. 23).

A letter by Dr. J. T. Gallagher in
the Boston Post of October 4 denounced
the first plays given by the Abbey
Players, Murray's Birthright and Lady
Gregory's Hyacinth Halvey, as vulgar,
unnatural, anti-national and anti-
Christian. Gallagher's soul cried out,
he wrote, "for a thousand tongues to
voice my unutterable horror and dis-
gust. . . . I never saw anything so
vulgar, vile, beastly, and unnatural,
so calculated to calumniate, degrade,
and defame a people and all they hold
sacred and dear" (Lady Gregory, p. 179).

On October 14, after the Boston
opening of The Playboy, the Gaelic

paraphrased
quotation and
direct quotation
—the direct
quotation was
retained because
of its language

notice the
ellipsis

<u>American</u> attacked the play in a page-one
article, with the following leader:

> Irishmen will stamp out <u>The</u> <u>Playboy</u>
> United Irish American societies. . . .
> Resolve To suppress, at any cost,
> the vile libel on Irish Womanhood
> and Gross Misrepresentation of
> their Religious feelings

The article resolved that nothing would
prevent the Irish-Americans from driving
the play from the stage, for they were
jealous of the good name of their race
and fully able to defend it. The real
offense of the word "shift" in <u>The</u>
<u>Playboy</u>, the article said, "was in
the plain intimation that in making
matrimonial matches it is common to line
up practically naked women for a suitor
to choose from."

A week later the paper charged <u>The</u>
<u>Playboy</u> was "an abomination and the
mind that conceived it was un-Irish
and incapable of understanding the real
mind of the people." The author and
all his defenders were called Anglo-
Irish, a charge that reflected the
Irish-Irish attitude of the Dublin
objectors. The Boston Irish societies
made the same objection to all the
Abbey plays, but in slightly more
picturesque language:

A Sample Research Paper

quoted directly,
because of the
language

Out of the 160 delegates to the
Central Council, 150 are peasants
or the sons of peasants. They know
their Ireland as children know their
mother, and they have no hesitation
in affirming that the vulgar,
raucous, ewehoughers and incendi-
aries, retching drunkards, degenerate
women, religious impostors, fratri-
cides and parricides depicted in
these alleged Irish plays no more
represent the peasantry of Ireland
than the Apaches of Paris or the
Thugs of India." (<u>Gaelic American</u>,
Nov. 4).

chronological
and geographical
order

In spite of these attacks and an
attempt to have the censor ban the
plays, there were no demonstrations in
the theater. The company felt the
American tour had started well, and
would be successful. From Boston the
company went to Providence, where a
deputation of Irish-Americans demanded
that another play be substituted for
<u>The Playboy</u>. Lady Gregory refused.
The Providence <u>Journal</u> (Nov. 2) reported
the plays as well received but poorly
attended. Two hundred customers and
fifty police saw <u>The Playboy</u>; the final
applause was almost an ovation (Lady
Gregory, p. 178).

In New Haven the Chief of Police,
acting as the official censor, attended
an afternoon rehearsal and demanded
that a list of cuts he had noted be

made in Synge's play before it could
go on in the evening. Since the Chief
had attended a rehearsal of Shaw's
<u>Blanco</u> <u>Posnet</u>, Lady Gregory gladly
complied (Lady Gregory, p. 187). One
assumes the Chief was gratified by not
hearing the passages to which he had
objected.

The company journeyed from New Haven
to Washington, D.C. Here they encountered the first organized opposition
by the Catholic Church. Two or three
priests denounced the plays from the
pulpit, and a pamphlet was distributed
at church doors by the Aloysius Truth
Society, protesting the performance:

> The attention of fair-minded
> Washingtonians is called to a most
> malignant travesty of Irish life
> and religion about to be presented
> upon the stage of a local theatre
> by the Irish Players.
> A storm of bitter protest has
> been raised in every city in which
> they have presented their false and
> revolting picture of Irish life.
> Dublin people never accepted the
> plays. . . .
> Among the vicious caricatures,
> one in particular is an open insult
> to every intelligent theatre-goer—
> <u>The</u> <u>Playboy</u> <u>of</u> <u>the</u> <u>Western</u> <u>World</u>.
> It contains blasphemous references
> to God and the most sacred objects
> of life (<u>Irish</u> <u>Independent</u>, Nov.
> 28, 1911).

In spite of the church opposition,

A Sample Research Paper

the plays were received without any
demonstrations.

Since the Gaelic-American societies
were organizing the demonstrations,
the Irish press reported the American
opposition, and Yeats was busy writing
to the Dublin papers giving favorable
reports of the play's reception, or
appearing on the Abbey stage speaking
of some city which had received the
plays and the players with respect
and attention: "Yeats came forward
and made a speech after the morality
The Interlude of Youth. He called those
who objected to The Playboy in America
Tom Fool Irishmen. He said that the
press in Ireland was giving a distorted
view of what was happening in America.
He said the plays were a success"
(Holloway, 1911, p. 783).

note how the
transition from
Ireland to
America is made
smoothly by the
use of the word
"success"

The plays were a success in New York,
if one simply counts the number of
people who came to the theater, for
whatever reason. The company expected
trouble in New York, the headquarters of
the Clan-naGael. John Quinn, a noted
lawyer, art collector, and patron of
Irish letters, who had been interested

in the Abbey from its inception, told
Lady Gregory he was afraid what might
happen when The Playboy was presented.
He felt certain that the Gaelic American's campaign would erupt violently,
for one of his friends in the Gaelic
movement had told him: "There is a party
of rowdies coming to the theatre tonight
to make their demonstrations." Lady
Gregory was urged to let the enemy know
that the company was prepared for some
demonstrations, and thus stop them
from coming, but she thought "it better
to let them show themselves. They have
been threatening so long; we shall see
who they are" (Lady Gregory
pp. 199-200).

The Playboy opened in New York on
November 27. The theater was packed and
a great number of police were present.
Trouble started in the middle of the
first act when a man in the audience
rose and cried, "Put 'em off!" Men
and women in the gallery and orchestra
jumped to their feet. There was a stream
of catcalls and hisses (Sun, Nov. 29).
Eggs, potatoes—everything available
was thrown at the stage. One man took

out his watch and fired it at one of
the actors, O'Donovan. An actress, Miss
McGee, was smacked on the head with a
potato. The police charged in and made
200 arrests, and the company attempted
to continue the play.[20] Lennox Robinson,
the Abbey's manager, was so incensed
at the demonstrators that he helped the
police throw the disturbers down the
marble staircase of the Maxine Elliott
Theatre.[21] During the demonstration,
according to the _World_ of November 28,
many noted people in the audience were
drenched with red pepper and asaphoetida,
a foul-smelling milky juice. Lady
Gregory, in the best stage tradition,
crouched behind the stage hearth,
encouraging the players to go only
through the motions and save their
voices. After the first act, when the
police had removed many of the demonstrators, O'Donovan announced from the
stage that the play would begin again,
and it did, to a delighted audience
(Lady Gregory, p. 203). The New York

---

[20]Holloway, Dec. 16, 1911, p. 984,
quoting a letter from an eyewitness,
Violet Chiappie.

[21]Robinson, p. 96.

Tribune, November 28, carried a full
report of the riots:

> There was a grand little riot
> at Maxine Elliott's theatre last
> night when the Irish players tried
> to produce The Playboy of the
> Western World. The players were
> busy enough at one stage of the game
> dodging potatoes, eggs, bread, and
> balls of asaphoetida—and they were
> busy all through dodging hoots,
> hisses, and cat-calls—but the police
> were busier throwing people out.
> More than a hundred were thrown
> out, and there were at least twenty
> fights and half a hundred near fights.
> Traffic lines were formed at
> Sixth Avenue and Broadway and crowds
> hung about the corners all the
> evening watching the show on the
> outside of the theatre, as man after
> man was hustled out by a bunch of
> husky cops. Three relays of reserves
> were hurried to the scene. . . .

The crowds outside the theater were
as bad as the rowdies inside, or perhaps
the rowdies who had been inside were
now outside. In any case, when the play
was concluded the actors had to be es-
corted home in taxis (Holloway,
1911, p. 984).

The next evening Teddy Roosevelt,
partly as a favor to Lady Gregory and
partly out of interest in the Abbey
Players and the plays, attended the
theater with John Quinn and Lady
Gregory. Chief of Police McAdoo, who
was sent by Mayor Gaynor to see the

A Sample Research Paper

play, was in the box with Roosevelt.
Chief McAdoo found nothing to censor
in The Playboy of the Western World,
and Roosevelt was so impressed that
he urged Quinn to write an article on
the company, saying that he would
print it in The Outlook. Quinn did,
and the article appeared (December 16)
with an introduction by Teddy Roosevelt.

The New York engagement was a great
financial success. The notoriety given
by the riots brought people to the
theater in great numbers. For the
same reason, the Philadelphia engagement was hugely successful. On Tuesday,
January 16, 1912, the company presented
The Playboy to a crowded house in
Philadelphia. The usual first-night
riot occurred. Not much was thrown at
the actors but a slice of currant cake,
which hit Arthur Sinclair, and one
or two eggs, which did not. Sinclair
said the eggs were fresh, an indication
of American prosperity that impressed
the company. Twenty-five people were
ejected and two arrested for assault
before the play could begin again (Lady
Gregory, p. 219).

transition from
New York to
Philadelphia

After this unmannerly reception, the city officials were determined to prevent the play from being given again. Lady Gregory was notified on Wednesday that The Playboy would have to be withdrawn or she would risk arrest. She replied that she would rather be arrested than allow anyone to censor a play for which she and others had fought so hard. John Quinn had come from New York to see the company in Philadelphia, and he accompanied Lady Gregory to the theater. They found the entire company technically arrested (under a law enacted the previous year on the eve of Sarah Bernhardt's visit, forbidding "immoral or indecent plays"); but the Police Chief, who was a friend, not only refused to allow his men to arrest the actors, but threatened to arrest anyone who came on the stage to do so. In the end, Quinn arranged to accept warrants for arrest, post bail bonds, and have the hearing put off until the following Friday.[29] The Playboy went

the information given here, while of interest, is not important enough for the body of the paper and is properly put in a footnote

[29] Lady Gregory, pp. 222-223. After some legal maneuvering, and the dramatic re-arrival of Quinn from New York during the questioning of a witness, the case was dismissed.

on. A force of three hundred police
assured the company they would be un-
disturbed. The play, and the company,
were a great success. Arthur Sinclair
wrote to Holloway: "Going great.
Making a sensation in Philadelphia.
Notices magnificent" (Holloway, Jan.
1912, p. 115).

The demonstrations against The
Playboy caused considerable comment
in Ireland. Yeats wrote that the arrest
of the Abbey Players would merely result
in giving the play another huge ad-
vertisement (Irish Times, Jan. 20).
Shaw's comment was a masterpiece of
satire:

> The occurrence is too ordinary
> to be worth comment. All decent
> people are arrested in America. That
> is the reason I have refused all
> invitations to go there. Besides,
> who am I to question Philadelphia's
> right to make itself ridiculous.
> I warned the Irish players that
> America, being governed largely by
> a mysterious race—probably one of
> the lost tribes of Israel, calling
> themselves American Gaels—is a
> dangerous country for genuine
> Irishmen and Irishwomen. The American
> Gaels are the real playboys of the
> Western World, and they are naturally
> angry with Synge for showing them
> up. . . . (Irish Independent, Jan. 20)

Such eminent criticism was difficult
for the Gaelic American to rebut, so
the paper changed the emphasis in its

note the constant
attempt to
emphasize the
connection be-
tween Ireland
and America

criticism from the play to the personalities supporting it:

> William Butler Yeats screaming
> lies across the broad Atlantic . . .
> is enough to frighten the fishes
> out of their wits. And why he gets
> so angry over what he calls "a
> splendid advertisement" is one of
> those things which we unfortunates
> "who have lost touch with Ireland"
> and are "thirty years behind the
> times" cannot understand. And
> George Bernard Oh Pshaw's verbal
> lambasting of the Clan-na-Gael and
> the American Gaels makes one wonder
> why a great man wastes his valuable
> time with such undramatic, untheatric
> blockheads.
>
> Lady Gregory contributes the
> only element of tragedy to the show.
> It is pitiable to see a woman of
> education and refinement who could
> find plenty of congenial work in
> the uplifting of the people among
> whom her lot is cast, making such a
> spectacle of herself in her old age
> trying to force a dirty and debasing
> play down the throats of an indignant
> and outraged people and posing as
> an authority on a subject of which
> she is as ignorant as she is of
> astronomy and trigonometry. And her
> feeble attempts to magnify little
> audiences into imposing assemblages
> of "celebrated people" are pitiful
> exhibitions of the result of taking
> the first false step.
>
> Wherever The Playboy goes the
> Irish people rise up in protest and
> make the drama that is absent from
> the dirty play. The drama is then
> transferred to the police station,
> the magistrate's court, and the
> newspaper office. Shaw, Yeats, and
> Lady Gregory are so ignorant of Irish
> character that they think police
> clubs, prison cells, and abusive
> language will accomplish here in
> America what these things and worse
> have failed to bring about in seven
> centuries in Ireland. The poor fools
> (Gaelic America, Jan. 2, 1912).

After Philadelphia, the company
went to Pittsburgh, to Indianapolis,
and then to Chicago. The farther west
the company went, the less violent
became the disturbances. In spite of
the resolution of Irish-Americans in
Chicago that they did not want the
play presented there (<u>Gaelic</u> <u>American</u>,
Feb. 3, 1912), and a threatening letter
with a picture of a coffin and pistol
that declared that Lady Gregory would
"never see the hills of Connemara
again" and was about to meet her
death, <u>The</u> <u>Playboy</u> ended its Chicago
run in such peace that Lady Gregory
"nearly fell asleep" (Gregory, p. 249).
One of the players wrote to Holloway:
"We did <u>The</u> <u>Playboy</u> here nearly every
night last week, and although some of
us (from what we had heard) expected
to be shot, there wasn't the slightest
disturbance of any kind . . . the
audiences were most enthusiastic"
(Holloway, Feb. 1912, p. 229).

There can be no doubt that there was
an understanding between the Irish-Irish
and the Irish-Americans who attempted

to suppress The Playboy. For the Irish
the play represented the influence
and dominance of the Irish Protestant,
traditionally English oriented; for
the Americans it presented, on the one
hand, a play that their Irish cousins
resented; on the other, a play through
which the Stage Irishman once again
plagued them across the footlights.
For Yeats and Lady Gregory, who were
the targets for all the abuse, the fight
was for "Freedom from mob censorship
. . . for the freedom of the artist to
choose his material from the whole
of life, and to deal with it as his art
required."

This fight for artistic freedom is
one that every generation must make
against the shibboleths that society
erects against the artist, his material,
and his medium.

note that this
concludes both
sections of the
paper and
repeats, with
variation, the
main thesis of
the paper

Selective Bibliography

Arrow, The. No. 3. Dublin, 1907.

Colum, Mary. Life and the Dream. New York, 1947.

Colum, Padraic. Road Round Ireland. New York, 1937.

Fay, William G. and Catherine Carswell. Fays of the Abbey Theatre. London, 1935.

Greene, David Herbert, and Edward Stephens. J. M. Synge, 1871-1909.

Gregory, Lady Isabelle Augusta. Our Irish Theatre. New York, 1913.

Henderson, W. A. Manuscript clipping books in the National Library, Dublin.

Holloway, Joseph. "A Dublin Playgoer's Impressions." Unpublished manuscript diaries in the National Library, Dublin.

Magee, William K. (John Eglinton, pseud.) Irish Literary Portraits. London, 1935.

O'Brien, Conor Cruise. Parnell and His Party. Oxford, 1957.

O'Hegarty, P. S. A History of Ireland Under the Union, 1801-1922. London, 1952.

Phillips, W. Alison. Revolution in Ireland. New York, 1923.

Revival of Irish Literature. Addresses by Sir Charles Gavan Duffy, Dr. George Sigerson, and Dr. Douglas Hyde. London, 1894.

Robinson, Lennox. Ireland's Abbey Theatre. London, 1951.

Yeats, William Butler. Dramatis Personae.

————. Letters, ed. Allen Wade. New York, 1954.

————. Plays and Controversies. London, 1923.

INDEX

Bantam Guides to Better English Usage

☐ 25552 **THE BANTAM CONCISE HANDBOOK OF ENGLISH** $3.95

An inexpensive handbook to better English usage with more easy-to-use advice on how to write clearly and effectively. The Bantam Handbook includes complete information on technical and business writing.

☐ 23933 **THE BANTAM INSTANT SPELLING HANDBOOK** $3.95

The Bantam Instant Spelling Handbook provides a comprehensive, easy-to-use list of over 20,000 words. It also offers special sections on basic spelling rules, a list of commonly misspelled words, a list of commonly confused words with their definitions, and memory games to help you remember easily words with difficult spellings.

Bantam has a complete reference library to fill your needs:

☐ 24145 **THE BANTAM BOOK OF CORRECT LETTER WRITING** $3.95
☐ 14344 **BUSINESS WRITING HANDBOOK** $3.95
☐ 26376 **WRITER'S SURVIVAL MANUAL** $4.50
☐ 26079 **WRITING & RESEARCHING TERM PAPERS** $3.50
☐ 22695 **WRITING IN GENERAL/THE SHORT STORY IN PARTICULAR** $2.95

Look for them at your bookstore or use this coupon for ordering:

Bantam Books, Inc., Dept. WR2, 414 East Golf Road,
Des Plaines, Ill. 60016

Please send me the books I have checked above. I am enclosing $_____
(please add $1.50 to cover postage and handling.) Send check or money order—no cash or C.O.D.s please.

Mr/Ms _____

Address _____

City/State _____ Zip _____

WR2—7/87

Please allow four to six weeks for delivery. This offer expires 1/88. Prices and availability subject to change without notice.

Bantam's
Language Arts Library

Special Offer
Buy a Bantam Book
for only 50¢.

Now you can have Bantam's catalog filled with hundreds of titles plus take advantage of our unique and exciting bonus book offer. A special offer which gives you the opportunity to purchase a Bantam book for only 50¢. Here's how!

By ordering any five books at the regular price per order, you can also choose any other single book listed (up to a $4.95 value) for just 50¢. Some restrictions do apply, but for further details why not send for Bantam's catalog of titles today!

Just send us your name and address and we will send you a catalog!